THE NIAGARA CONFERENCE LECTURES

POST TENEBRAS LUX

— ✦ —

Light after Darkness

CONTRIBUTORS

Kasey Horvath, Steven R. Martins, Theodore Van Raalte,
David Robinson, and Brian G. Najapfour

cantaroinstitute.org

Post Tenebras Lux: Light after Darkness Published by
Cántaro Publications, a publishing imprint of the
Cántaro Institute, 3248 Twenty-First St., Jordan
Station, ON. L0R 1S0

Book design by Paul Aurich

Library & Archives Canada
ISBN 978-1-998711-11-6

Printed in the United States of America

Table of Contents

Introduction
Post Tenebras Lux:
Light after Darkness

———————

THE PROTESTANT REFORMATION WAS not merely a rupture in Western ecclesiastical histor—it was a sovereign act of renewal that re-centered the church upon the authority of God's Word and the unmerited grace of the gospel. The phrase *Post Tenebras Lux*—"After Darkness, Light"—emerged as a defining motto of this movement, expressing the conviction that divine truth, though often eclipsed, cannot be extinguished. Light pierces the darkness. And in every age, it is God who dispels error by the illuminating power of His Word.

This conviction remains no less relevant today. The Reformation was not the culmination of reform but its enduring catalyst. The Niagara Conference 2024, hosted by the Cántaro Institute in Jordan Station, Ontario, Canada, was devoted to this very theme: *Post Tenebras Lux—Light after Darkness*. It called the church to remember what God has done and to reckon with what He still requires. The lectures gathered in this volume do not merely look backward; they speak prophetically into the present—reaffirming the timeless truths of Scripture and summoning Christ's people to courageous, confessional, and reformational faithfulness.

What the Reader Can Expect
In "Learning Confession and Repentance with the Psalms and Reformers," Rev. Kasey Horvath opened the conference with a pastoral

and doctrinal reflection on the nature of true repentance. Rooted in Psalm 51 and Martin Luther's 95 Theses, this lecture recovers the Reformational emphasis that repentance is not merely an emotional response or verbal admission but a comprehensive turning of the heart and life toward God. Horvath carefully distinguishes the biblical categories of contrition, confession, and repentance, showing how each reflects genuine faith and is indispensable to the Christian life. With clarity and conviction, he exhorts believers—pastors, parents, and parishioners alike—to recover a biblical, experiential, and reformational understanding of penitence that is both deeply personal and urgently needed in today's ecclesial and cultural moment.

In the second lecture, Rev. Steven R. Martins delves into "The Spanish Reformation", presenting a compelling historiographical and theological recovery of a Reformation often overlooked in both Protestant and Catholic narratives. Though crushed institutionally by the Inquisition, the Spanish Reformation produced men of deep theological insight and spiritual courage—figures such as Julian Hernández, Constantino Ponce de la Fuente, Casiodoro de Reina, and Cipriano de Valera. With precision and pastoral clarity, Martins traces the intellectual legacy and missionary zeal of these reformers, especially through their work in translating, proclaiming, and defending the gospel in the Spanish tongue. He situates their faithfulness within the broader context of Semper Reformanda, calling the contemporary church to recover the same zeal for biblical fidelity, doctrinal clarity, and courageous witness. Though the Spanish Reformation was forced into exile, it was never extinguished—and its enduring voice continues to echo today through the Reina-Valera Bible and the growing resurgence of Reformed faith in the Spanish-speaking world.

Dr. Ted Van Raalte's "The Reformation in Europe" presents the European Reformation as a sovereign work of God's grace—uniting diverse peoples, languages, and regions in a shared return to the authority of Scripture. Rather than a fragmented or sectarian movement, the Reformation was a truly catholic (universal) renewal of Christ's one Church, as local reformers across Europe rediscovered the gospel and reformed doctrine and worship according to the Word of God. Through the lives of three French-speaking Reformed figures—Guillaume Farel, Guido de Brès, and Antoine de Chandieu—Van Raalte traces the Reformation's spiritual depth, doctrinal clarity, and theological maturity over time. Each figure, shaped by their era, exemplifies a commitment to the supremacy and sufficiency of Scripture, the centrality of Christ, and the comfort of sovereign grace. The lecture concludes by affirming that the Reformation, far from being a merely historical event, was a gracious and providential work of God to restore the gospel to His Church.

In "The Principle of Sola Scriptura," Dr. David Robinson explores the theological significance of the sixteenth-century correspondence between Lutheran theologians and Patriarch Jeremiah II of Constantinople, a rare yet illuminating exchange between the Protestant and Eastern Orthodox traditions. At the heart of the dialogue was a fundamental disagreement over the nature of religious authority: while both parties revered the Scriptures, the Reformers affirmed Scripture alone as the ultimate and sufficient rule of faith and practice, in contrast to the Orthodox insistence on the interpretive authority of ecclesial tradition and the ecumenical councils. Through this historical encounter, Robinson underscores the enduring relevance of *sola scriptura*—not merely as a polemical stance against Rome, but as a principled return to the clarity, sufficiency, and supremacy of God's Word in the life of the church.

Lastly, Dr. Brian G. Najapfour's lecture, "The Principle of Soli Deo Gloria," expounds the Reformation's ultimate theological aim: the glory of God alone in all things. Anchored in Romans 11:36, Najapfour demonstrates that this principle is not merely a pious motto but the necessary consequence of the other Reformation *so-*

las—Scripture alone, grace alone, faith alone, and Christ alone. In contrast to Rome's synergistic soteriology, which shares glory between God and man, the Reformers rightly confessed that salvation is entirely *from* God, *through* God, and *unto* God. As Najapfour traces *Soli Deo Gloria*'s biblical foundation and doctrinal implications, he underscores that God is the source, agent, and goal of all redemptive work. This vision of divine supremacy fosters humility, assurance, and a life lived unto the praise of God's glorious grace. Whether in salvation or vocation, worship or suffering, the cry of the Reformation remains our own: *Soli Deo Gloria*.

Conclusion

Taken together, the lectures in this volume do more than retrace the contours of the sixteenth-century Reformation—they present a robust theological framework for faithfully navigating the present. Each contribution, in its own way, reminds us that the Reformation was not a closed chapter of church history but an ongoing summons to return to the Word of God, to cling anew to the gospel of grace, and to live entirely for the glory of God.

The task of reformation is never complete. As long as the church sojourns in a fallen world, it must continually examine itself in the light of Scripture, resist the allure of worldly compromise, and cultivate a spirit of repentance, humility, and doctrinal clarity. It must speak with courage, live with integrity, and worship with reverence—anchored in the same truths that turned the upside-down world right side up five centuries ago.

In that enduring Reformational spirit, this volume is offered: to instruct the mind, strengthen the conscience, and call Christ's people to steadfast faithfulness in the midst of darkness.

Soli Deo Gloria.

Editorial Team
Cántaro Publications

Learning Confession and Repentance with the Psalms and Reformers

Rev. Kasey Horvath

Well, good evening, and grace and peace to you all.

My church is part of a Protestant denomination, as Ryan just alluded—*The Communion of Reformed Evangelical Churches*. As the pastor of a Presbyterian and Reformed church, it is my joy to commemorate and reflect on our shared Protestant heritage with you this evening.

The title of this conference, *Light After Darkness*, is a phrase John Calvin used to describe the profound spiritual reform that occurred in the city of Geneva. This conference, *Light After Darkness*, seeks to honor God's work in the Protestant Reformation and invites us to consider what lessons from our Reformed heritage remain useful, profitable, and instructional today. What is useful? What is profitable? What is instructional from the Reformation? In light of this, the title of my lecture is *Learning Confession and Repentance with the Psalms and Reformers*. My goal this evening is to provide a biblical explanation of confession and repentance, focusing on Psalm 51, while also highlighting the importance of confession and repentance during the Protestant Reformation—particularly as seen in Martin Luther's *95 Theses*, famously nailed to the door of Castle Church in Wittenberg, Germany, on October 31, 1517.

Now, you may be thinking, "Pastor Kasey, out of all the doctrines associated with the Protestant Reformation, why choose to speak about confession and repentance?" Well, as I just mentioned, this was a doctrine of great importance to the Reformers. Thus, any effort to honor the Protestant Reformation must address this theological teaching to some extent. However, beyond its historical significance, there are deeper implications to consider. I am particularly concerned with the practical implications of understanding and applying the doctrine of confession and repentance in our present day—*in this cultural moment,* if you will. The practical relevance of this doctrine is both significant and far-reaching, which is why I have chosen it as the focus of my lecture.

You see, if we Reformed Christians are going to call the secular culture to repentance—(and we should)—we must be able to clearly articulate what we are calling them to do. Likewise, for those of us who are pastors, as we preach and counsel from the Word, pleading with our parishioners to reconcile with God, it is both good and right to provide our hearers with clear instructions on how to do so. Also, for those of us who are parents raising our children in the fear and admonition of the Lord, it is essential to teach our kids the significance of confession and repentance. This is not just important—it is profoundly practical in shaping their understanding of walking faithfully with God.

It has often been said that faith and repentance are two sides of the same coin—when faith is truly experienced, repentance will follow. Similarly, when repentance is demonstrated, it reveals that faith has already been exercised. This evening, as I highlight the technical aspects of confession and repentance, I want to be very clear: I am operating with the presupposition that justification—being declared "not guilty"—is by grace alone, through faith alone, in Christ alone. The penal and substitutionary atoning work of Jesus Christ on the cross is the only means by which a person is justified before God and saves him from God's wrath and just judgment. It is faith, wrought by the Holy Spirit, that applies the atoning work of Christ to the sinner, making him righteous and granting him the riches of Christ Jesus. Everything I say tonight about confession and repentance presupposes that faith is essential for true repentance because repentance is an expression of true faith. Jesus our Lord Himself preached this very message: "Repent and believe the gospel" (Mark 1:15). So then, with all that being said, let us now turn to the Psalms and the Reformers to learn about confession and repentance.

The Bible outlines three essential components of true repentance

- **Contrition:** How I Feel About Sin
- **Confession:** What I say About Sin
- **Repentance:** What I Do in Response to Sin

All three of these elements are evident in Psalm 51. It is important to note, these three elements of penitence – contrition, confession, and repentance—are also evident in Martin Luther's 95 Theses. Therefore, we will consider Psalm 51 and Luther's 95 Theses in tandem, as we learn about confession and repentance.

Contrition: How I Feel About Sin

Let's begin by examining the first essential component of penitence: contrition—how I feel about sin. Listen to Psalm 51:8, 12, and 17:

> Let me hear joy and gladness, but the bones that you have
> broken rejoice, (v. 8)
> Restore to me the joy of your salvation and
> uphold me with a willing spirit (v. 12).
> The sacrifices of God are a broken spirit,
> a broken and *contrite* heart.
> O God, you will not despise (v. 17).

The Hebrew language in verse 17 conveys the idea of feeling emotionally crushed under the weight of guilt, shame, and remorse. This verse reflects a heart posture that feels deeply broken over sin—a vital component of true penitence. In modern-day Presbyterian and Reformed circles, we often avoid discussing emotions or feelings. This aversion exists because, over many decades, Western psychology and secular thought have elevated feelings and emotions as supreme, making them the standard by which all truth claims are measured. This shift has caused numerous societal and cultural problems, including the absurd notion of "my truth" versus *the* truth. In response to the error that emotions are supreme, Reformed Christians have rightly asserted that God is supreme. His Word, revealed in the Bible, is the ultimate standard by which all things are measured—not your feelings or mine. This is the correct and necessary response. But in reacting to the sinful exaltation of human emotions, we have mistakenly overlooked the fact that God created us as emotional beings. This overreaction has resulted in an unnecessary aversion to discussing emotions—an approach that, I would argue, is neither good nor healthy. He has given us emotions to be used for our good and for His glory. A biblical study of sackcloth and ashes reveals that God's people have historically expressed their emotions profoundly, especially in response to sin.

A cursory look at the Bible reveals God's people weeping, tearing their garments, wearing sackcloth, and heaping ashes to express their deep emotions, as illustrated in Psalm 51:17. This reflects the feeling of being emotionally crushed under the weight of guilt, shame, and remorse, as described in Psalm 51:17. In Psalm 32:3–4, King David describes the anguish of being broken under the weight of guilt and shame, *"When I kept silent, my bones wasted away through my groaning all day long. For day and night your hand was heavy upon me; my strength was dried up as by the heat of summer."*

Contrition is a vital component of true penitence because it demonstrates the work of the Holy Spirit in bringing conviction of sin and is the fruit of a sensitive conscience that has not been hardened. Contrition is a very practical way of expressing the proper response to sin: one should feel ashamed, experience guilt, and express remorse.

Martin Luther's famous *95 Theses* were formally titled *A Disputation on the Power and Efficacy of Indulgences.* All 95 Theses were written to combat and correct the false papal teaching that sins could be pardoned through the selling and buying of indulgences, directly opposing the false gospel of purchasing letters of pardon. In Theses 35 and 40, the Reformer asserted that contrition is an essential component of true penitence. Luther even argued that one could wrongly buy indulgences without ever feeling *truly remorseful*. Martin Luther believed that a lack of contrition pointed to an insincere desire to seek forgiveness for sin. Of course, he did not arrive at this conclusion on his own—his criticism of buying indulgences was firmly rooted in theology drawn from the pages of Scripture.

As we have seen in Psalm 51:17, contrition—how I feel about sin—is the first technical component of penitence. Now, let's turn our attention to the second component: *confession*—what I say about sin.

Confession: What I Say About Sin

Listen to Psalm 51:1–7:

> Have mercy on me, O God.
> > According to your steadfast love,
> > according to your abundant mercy,
> > blot out my transgressions.
> Wash me thoroughly from my iniquity,
> and cleanse me from my sin.
> For I know my transgressions,
> and my sin is ever before me.
> Against you and you only have I seen and
> > done what is evil in your sight,
> so that you might be justified in your words
> and blamelessin your judgments.
> Behold, I was brought forth in iniquity,
> and in sin did my mother conceive me.
> Behold, you delight in truth in the inward being.
> You teach me wisdom in the secret hearts.
> Purge me with hyssop, and I shall be clean.
> Wash me, and I shall be whiter than snow.

Contrition is how I feel about sin; it involves feeling the weight of being emotionally crushed by guilt, shame, and remorse. Confession, on the other hand, is what I say about sin. In these seven verses, David makes two key statements about his own sin.

First, David acknowledged his wrongdoing—he admitted to sinning against God's law without making excuses or shifting blame. He took full responsibility for his transgression, confessing that he had sinned against God and violated His law. David sinned against people, but he recognized that his ultimate offense was against God's statutes. Thus, David does not downplay the impact of his sin on people but recognized that the greatest violation was against God. This is the first key statement David makes – ownership of wrongdoing.

The second thing David verbally communicates is a plea for mercy. In verses 1, 2, and 7, David petitions God for His mercy, which would wash and cleanse him from sin. Confession is a vital component of repentance because, through confession, we are washed clean by the blood of Jesus. This is precisely what the Apostle John stated in his first epistle, *"If we confess our sins, God is faithful and just to forgive us our sins and to cleanse us from all unrighteousness"* (1 John 1:9). Thus, David took responsibility for his sin through *confession* and pleaded with God for *cleansing*.

Now, there are two ways we experience confession and cleansing. First, we come to Jesus in faith and experience justification. In that moment of justification, the heart knows and acknowledges its sin, along with the subsequent need for God's mercy. Therefore, faith is exercised with the pretense that one is a sinner who has violated God's law and is in need of God's mercy. Just as David expressed in Psalm 51, this initial confession and cleansing can be described as *forensic* righteousness. By grace through faith in Christ, we confess our sins, and in doing so, we experience the cleansing blood of Jesus, through which God declares us not guilty. There is a confession of sin and a cleansing from sin, both of which we experience in justification when we come to Christ in faith. This is the first way we experience confession and cleansing.

The second way we experience this is as adopted sons and daughters of God in sanctification, what I like to call *functional* righteousness. Christians do sin, and when we do, the Bible commands us to repent and feel contrition for our sin. The Bible also calls us to confess our sin. Saint John makes this point clear in *1 John 2:1–2, "My little children, I am writing these things to you so that you may not sin. But if anyone does sin, we have an advocate with the Father, Jesus Christ the righteous. He is the propitiation for our sins."* When a son or daughter of God sins, they confess their sin to restore right fellowship with their Heavenly Father.

For example, my sons and daughters are biologically my children. When they disobey me, they do not lose their biological makeup, nor do they lose their standing in my house as my children. Therefore, when I discipline them, I am not trying to make them my children all over again. Instead, I am teaching and correcting them as my sons and daughters. Likewise, when my children confess their disobedience, they are not re-entering our family all over again. Instead, they are acknowledging their wrongdoing and asking for forgiveness to restore a right relationship with me, their father. This is what Saint John described in his epistle and what the author of Hebrews explained in Hebrews 12. God disciplines His sons and daughters, when they sin, to correct and teach them. Furthermore, God's children confess their sins, not to receive justification again but to grow in their sanctification, as adopted and beloved children of God. Therefore, we acknowledge our wrongdoing and seek the Father's forgiveness so that we may be cleansed and restored to fellowship with Him.

Confession is a vital component of penitence because, through confession, you and I are washed clean by the blood of Jesus—both in forensic righteousness and in functional righteousness.

In the context of opposing the false teaching of buying and selling indulgences, Martin Luther asserted in Theses 5 through 7 that the Pope cannot truly forgive sins—only God can. Furthermore, throughout his disputation, Luther argued against the notion of cleansing power of paid pardons. Of course, the reasoning behind the Reformers protest was the theological truth that cleansing and pardon from sin can only be experienced through faith when one confesses their sins to God.

This is the second technical component of true penitence: confession—what I say about sin. Now, let's consider the third element: repentance—what I do in response to sin

Repentance: What I Do in Response to Sin

Listen to Psalm 51:13:

"Then I will teach transgressors your ways,
and sinners will return to you."

When Christians speak about repentance, they often do so without understanding its precise, technical meaning. Sometimes people speak of repentance as feeling remorse for their sin or feeling bad—perhaps even guilt or shame. However, as we've already discovered, how I feel about sin is contrition; it is not repentance. Likewise, others use the word *repentance* to mean asking for forgiveness, apologizing, or admitting they're wrong. But, as we've already learned, what I say about sin—particularly my sin—is confession, and that is not repentance.

So, then you might ask, what is repentance? If it's not feeling sorry for yourself or feeling sorry about your sin; if it's not apologizing; if it's not asking for forgiveness—what, then, is repentance? The biblical definition of repentance is a change of heart and mind that results in a change of behavior. This is demonstrated by John the Baptist's words to the Pharisees, "Bear fruit in keeping with repentance" (Matt. 3:8). You see, a person with a changed heart and mind bears fruit that reflects that inward transformation.

This change of heart and its practical fruit are what David expresses in Psalm 51. After feeling guilt for his sin and experiencing God's mercy, David committed to an actionable and measurable change in his life. He stated that he would do something different from sin—something in contrast to his sin. The primary act of repentance for David in Psalm 51 was to turn away from sin by turning toward the vocation of teaching and instructing sinners in God's ways (Psalm 51:13).

When discussing true penitence, it is crucial for the church to articulate repentance accurately, distinguishing it from expressing guilt or confessing sin. It is good and right for our pastors, as well as our brothers and sisters in the Lord, to expect measurable change in our lives. Likewise, as we call the culture to repentance, it is logical for us to expect change in others. Furthermore, it is reasonable to expect measurable change in behavior when we call our children to repent and to hold them accountable for those changes.

Now, you may ask, is that biblical? Do we have justification for holding people accountable to change? The answer is yes—it is biblical. In Ephesians 4:17–32, the Apostle Paul teaches the importance of putting off sin and putting on righteousness. In other words, he emphasized the necessity of measurable behavioral change. According to the Apostle Paul, repentance for a thief involves more than contrition and confession—it requires putting off the sin of theft and putting on the righteous act of giving to the needy (Ephesians 4:28). In short, for the thief, bearing fruit in keeping with repentance means getting a job so he can give to the needy.

Likewise, Saint Paul called Christians to measurable change, in which their behavior could be observed, by analyzing whether one lashes out in anger or chooses to speak the truth in love (Ephesians 4:31).

According to Saint Paul, repentance is a two-part behavioral change. In repentance one completes a negative action in which they *put off* sin (Ephesians 4:22). While simultaneously exercising a positive action by *putting on* righteousness (Ephesians 4:24). What Saint Paul commands is measurable, objective behavioral change. Therefore, expecting others to change and expecting ourselves to change is biblical—it is an essential part of repentance. This is why the Apostle Paul could say to the Corinthians, after listing many sinful behaviors, "Such *were* some of you" (1 Corinthians 6:11). He spoke in the past tense because the Corinthians had experienced a change of heart and mind. They experienced the grace of the gospel at work within them, and they changed their behavior. God expects us to change, and He empowers us through the Holy Spirit to be transformed into the likeness of His Son.

The gospel is good news—good news that we can be saved through Jesus, but it is also good news that you and I can be transformed by Him. Many people are content with being saved by Jesus, but they show little interest in becoming like Him. And yet, throughout Scripture, we are consistently called to follow in the footsteps of our Lord, take up our cross, and follow Him. We are urged to follow the apostles' teaching as they follow Christ. The New Testament consistently teaches that we are to become like our Lord. This process of becoming like Jesus is what we call Sanctification.

Martin Luther understood the doctrine of repentance - at the very beginning of his disputation, he shattered our inaccurate modern understanding and usage of the word repentance. In Thesis 1, Martin Luther stated: "Our Lord and Master Jesus Christ, when He said 'repent,' willed that the whole life of believers should be repentance." With this statement, Luther captured the essence of the doctrine of sanctification. Christianity is the daily work of reorienting one's life to the Word inscribed and the Word incarnate. In Thesis 3, Martin Luther further stated, *"Yet it means not inward repentance only* (we might say contrition and confession). Yet, there is no true inward repentance that does not outwardly produce a diverse mortification of the flesh". According to Luther, diverse mortification of the flesh is repentance. In other words, repentance is a change of behavior. Again, Martin Luther didn't develop this concept on his own. In his thesis and disputation against the selling of indulgences and their supposed efficacy, as he discusses repentance, he draws on a theology rooted in Scripture. This theology aligns with the Apostle Paul's command to mortify the flesh—to kill sin—which is behavioral change. You are called to put to death the deeds of the flesh so that you might put on the deeds of righteousness. In short, you are called to change and become more like Jesus Christ.

This evening, as we've considered repentance, I hope you see that it is a vital component of penitence, as it reflects a true change of heart and mind.

Furthermore, as we have explored confession and repentance through the Psalms and the Reformers, I hope you will feel and express contrition toward sin, recognizing it as both biblical and essential – it is biblical to feel broken and contrite and to express those emotions. Luther maintained that a lack of contrition indicated an insincere desire for forgiveness.

Additionally, my desire is that, in faith, you would confess your sins to God. Again, in his *95 Theses*, Luther's main argument was that the Pope cannot truly forgive sin, as that is solely the work of God—only God can forgive sin. And so, as we reflect on the doctrine of confession and repentance, I pray that you will confess your sins to God and experience the cleansing power of Jesus' atoning blood.

Also, I pray that you would not only desire to be saved by Jesus, but also to be transformed into His likeness. Because repentance is a change of heart and mind manifested in a change of behavior.

I pray that, after reflecting on confession and repentance in the context of the Psalms and the Reformers, you would embrace these truths in your walk with God. I pray that you would experience faith and repentance in the name of the Father, and of the Son, and of the Holy Spirit. Amen.

All references to Martin Luther's Ninety-Five Theses are from the revised edition of "Martin Luther's 95 Theses: Disputation of Doctor Martin Luther on the Power and Efficacy of Indulgences" © 2016 Concordia Publishing House 3558 S. Jefferson Ave., St. Louis, MO 63118-3968

Scripture quotations are from the ESV Bible® (The Holy Bible, English Standard Version®), copyright © 2001 by Crossway Bibles, a publishing ministry of Good News Publishers. Used by permission. All rights reserved.

All Saints Presbyterian Church, New Holland, PA, USA.
www.allsaints-church.com

The Spanish Reformation

REV. STEVEN R. MARTINS

Introductory Remarks

LAST EVENING WE HAD the privilege of having Rev. Kasey Horvath with us to open our conference. He spoke on "Learning Confession and Repentance with the Psalms and Reformers." Such a pastoral and personable lecture served as a most fitting introduction to our conference: *Post Tenebras Lux*, Light After Darkness. It has been our vision, on this occasion, to look back upon our protestant history, to learn of God's past doings, and what we can learn for our living *Coram Deo* today. Every session of our conference has a distinct focus, and I have the privilege to address you today on a most neglected and misunderstood aspect of our protestant history, the Spanish reformation.

Admittedly, to suggest that the Spanish reformation has been a neglected and misunderstood aspect does appear to be, at its surface, an unqualified, blanket statement. You can, after all, find a select number of publications on the history of Spanish Protestantism, but when you compare how much has been written on the subject, whether as journal articles, dissertations, etc., to how much has been written on Protestantism in Germany, The Netherlands, or even England, it becomes apparent that on the one side you have a small puddle to jump into, whereas on the other side you have the water reservoir of the Hoover Dam. What accounts for this particular differential lies in part in the conventional narrative surrounding the history and religious character of Spain. Sixteenth-century Spain, after all, was known for its Catholic religious fervor, its Inquisitorial office, and the *autos-de-fe*. One could reasonably ask, "Can anything good and protestant come from Catholic Spain?" But such a narrative is not one solely constructed by those outside looking in, it is also proudly upheld by the Spanish people.

History or Myth?

In the 1923 publication of the *Enciclopedia Universal Ilustrada*, translated as the Universal Illustrated Encyclopedia, the reformation in Spain is dismissed as something non-existent.[1] It states that its influence was minimal at best due to the prior Catholic reforms of Francisco Jimenez de Cisneros (1436-1517), a Spanish cardinal and Grand Inquisitor. It also states that such a reformation was doomed from the start due to the deeply-rooted and irrefutable Romanism of the time. And lastly, it states that any whiff of the Reformation was stamped out by the Spanish Inquisition. And while the extinguishment of such Spanish Protestantism is certainly vastly exaggerated, there is no denying that the Inquisition was like an octopus with widespread tentacles, extending as far to the New World in the Americas and the Philippines.

The very idea that the reformation never occurred in Spain is, at face value, erroneous. There was, in fact, a movement; most notably in two cities which were considered early protestant centres, those being Sevilla and Valladolid. According to the late English scholar Arthur Gordon Kindle, the reformation movement began:

> ...in the 1540s and continued through the 1550s, but was completely stamped out by the Inquisition in the early 1560s. This movement had its origins both in native cur-

---

1. *Enciclopedia Universal Ilustrada*, L (1923) entry under "Reforma."

rents of evangelical thought and anti-Roman feelings, and also in ideas imported from Erasmus and main-stream Reformers through literary and political contacts with more northerly countries.[2]

Peninsula Ibérica 1600

To be historically and contextually precise, the Spanish reformation did come to an end in the early 1560s, if we are referring specifically to the movement within Spanish borders. However, if we are referring to the reformation of God's Spanish-speaking church, which had been exiled from her motherland, that reformation has in fact never come to an end. Instead, in keeping with the Reformational phrase *Semper Reformanda*, the church has continually sought to be reformed according to the teachings of God's Word. Now, it may not

2. A. Gordon Kindle, *Casiodoro de Reina: Spanish Reformer of the Sixteenth Century* (London, UK.: Tamesis Books Limited, 1975), xv.

be obvious in the broader Spanish-speaking church today, particularly with the ample dispersion of Arminianism, amongst as well the incursion of several false doctrines, there has always been a faithful remnant of Reformed Spanish Protestants who have sought this on-going reformation, and it has been quite recently that we have been seeing a resurgence and flourishment of the doctrines of grace more faithfully preached and applied.[3]

Biographic Profiles

Now, if what I have said so far suffices for an introduction to our subject – and one must bear in mind that this subject matter of the Spanish Reformation would require *more* than just a Saturday morning lecture – I wish to now walk us through some select biographic profiles of these Spanish reformers. And in this way, what we will have are several glimpses into what was the Spanish reformation. Glimpses of a greater panorama, pieces of a greater mosaic, snippets of a larger, more complex narrative.

Julian (Julianillo) Hernández

The first to be graced with such an honour is a relatively humble printer's apprentice who is not known for his writing but rather for the great risks he undertook to smuggle in protestant works into Spain. His name is Julian Hernández, familiarly known by his contemporaries as Julianillo, which on the one hand was a term of endearment, and on the other hand was in reference to his thin frame, being nothing more than skin and bone. We are not told how he became a protestant, but we can only imagine that his work as a printer's apprentice, while outside of Spain, acquainted him with several Lutheran works. And at some point

---

3. Miguel Núñez, "La Reforma Protestante." *Integridad y Sabiduría.* Accessed on February 2, 2018, http://integridadysabiduria.org la-reforma-protestante/.

prior to 1550, he not only embraced the true and biblical faith, but also a profound conviction to smuggle copies "of the Spanish Scriptures and other Reformed literature into Spain."[4] As The Banner of Truth's *J. MacPherson* writes:

> The Jesuit writer, Santiváñez, complains that Julianillo "with incredible skill discovered secret entrances and exits, and the poison of the new heresy spread rapidly throughout all Castille and Andalusia ... He himself taught men and women in the evil doctrines of the reformers, attaining his aim all too successfully." Julianillo's main deposit for the books he smuggled, hidden in wine casks, was the San Isidro monastery, and from there he travelled in a variety of disguises to place the books in the eager hands stretched out to receive them.[5]

This particularly dangerous work of smuggling Scriptures and Reformed literature into a nation that for the most part prohibited the Scriptures in the common tongue of the people, and which loathed all things Reformed, took place between the years 1550 and 1559. Amongst the works he brought in were the New Testament translations of Juan Perez de Pineda. When one considers the laborious groundwork that Julianillo engaged in, it would be no exaggeration to say that without Julianillo's efforts, the protestant centers of Valladolid and Seville would have suffered. Given the religio-cultural context, the recovery of the biblical gospel, of God's truth, could only have been possible with the Word of God in the common tongue, and Julianillo was the instrument that God providentially used to bring the Scriptures to the commoner's hands.

---

4. J. MacPherson, "The Reformation in Spain: Its Suppression", *The Christian Study Library*. Accessed on November 5, 2024, https://www.christianstudylibrary.org/article/reformation-spain-its-suppression/.

5. Ibid.

Eventually, Julianillo was caught. Most likely he was betrayed by someone who had feigned interest in his smuggled contents. And standing before the *Tribunal del Santo Oficio de la Inquisicion*, which was located in Seville, he was condemned and tortured in the most barbarous methods. MacPherson writes that at the hands of the Inquisition, Julianillo was tortured for approximately *three* whole years. In the end, after having dislocated several of his limbs, Julianillo was brought out to be burned at the stake for all to see. While we do not have a date for his birth, we do have a date for his martyrdom, December 22, 1560. Having endured what this humble man had endured, we would not have imagined his final words. He did not meet death with a whimper, nor regret. Even in the midst of the most excruciating pain, he sang aloud so that all the public could hear. What was it that he sung? What was that carol that so angered his persecutors? It was this:

¡Vencidos van los frailes, vencidos van! Corridos van los
    lobos, corridos van.

Which meant, translated to English, "The friars go vanquished, they go vanquished! The wolves go running, running they go." Why do you think Julianillo had been tortured for three years? He had been tortured in hopes that he would recant, that he would plead clemency, and find comfort in the penitence that the Catholic church offered him. The fact that he had been brought to the stake for all Seville to see was a clear testament of his unbreakable faith and conviction. This humble printer's apprentice, smuggler of Scriptures and Reformed literature, endured the Inquisitorial agents and the friars who supposedly knew the Scriptures all the better than he. His death, he perceived, was nothing more than his persecutor's admitting defeat. They could not undo God's work of salvation in his heart.

Why did I begin with Julianillo? Because those whom I am about to mention owe a great debt to the work of Julianillo. It was *because* of Julianillo that they had several protestant works in their hands, including provisional Spanish translations of the New Testament. And with such literary works, they were able to do the Lord's work with greater fidelity and precision. I am reminded of the apostle Paul's writings to the church in Rome:

> How then will they call on him in whom they have not believed? And how are they to believe in him of whom they have never heard? And how are they to hear without someone preaching? And how are they to preach unless they are sent? As it is written, "How beautiful are the feet of those who preach the good news!" (Rom. 10:14-15).

What beautiful feet were those of Julianillo.

The Observantine Hieronymites

If you remember, I had cited how one of the principal locations where Julianillo delivered his barrels-full of Scriptures and protestant works was the monastery of San Isidro. It was very much a protestant missionary center. This monastery was located a few miles northwest of Sevilla, and it was home to a religious order called *The Observantine Hieronymites*. I will refrain from speaking too much about the particular order and its influence because it remains today a subject of on-going study, but according to scholar Lewis J. Hutton, it was a religious order that, with the influence of the Reformed faith, held the potential to deeply influence the culture and development of Spain.[6] And the reason for this lies in that, contrary to the medieval Scholastic tendency to regard all things spiritual as superior to the earthly, this particular order held in high regard the common work of men and how this might be perceived as integral to man's worship of God. Hutton referred to it as a distinctive Spanish spirituality, a preliminary but certainly very raw form of what we today call the

---

6.   Lewis J. Hutton, "The Spanish Heretic: Cipriano de Valera", *Church History*, Cambridge University Press, Vol. 27, No. 1 (March, 1958), 23.

"protestant work ethic", something which would later emerge from the protestant reformation thanks to reformers like Martin Luther and John Calvin, to name two prominent figures.

Well, as the reformation spread throughout Europe, reformed ideas reached the monastery in the 1550s. And it did not take long until there was a significant number who had embraced the Reformed faith. Of course, given the nature of their religious order and where they were located, they were not what you might call *outward* protestants. They knew well the perils of the Spanish Inquisition, and that the Inquisition had not yet turned its full gaze towards what was happening within Spain. Now, for the sake of context, it was around this time that the Inquisition was faced with an *identity* crisis. Since it had been instituted, the Inquisition had sought the religious purity of Spain by converting, expelling, or executing Jews and Muslims, but by this time neither Judaism nor Islam were perceived as internal threats. You could say that it was a predatorial institution without any substantive prey, chasing after minor sects such as those of the *Alumbrados* who were a hodgepodge of Catholic, Lutheran, and mystical gnostic influences. When it became clear that Protestantism was alive and well *in Spain*, and threatening to alter the religio-cultural status quo, the Inquisition found its solution to its identity crisis. And clinging to their new-found purpose, no part of the global Spanish Empire would be deemed too far to extend its reach and to administer its misperceived "justice." Before this in-land protestant discovery, however, those who embraced the Reformed faith in the monastery held a deep desire to disseminate Scriptural truth all across Spain, and not just Spain, but the New World as well. At about this time, Spain was active in establishing settlements and colonies in the Americas. They had already engaged with the indigenous population, and many Catholic church leaders were operating missions in their midst, attempting to Christianize them in accordance to the

norms and standards of Rome. Evidence of this desire to disseminate Reformed literature to the New World is a translated Spanish
Bible dated to the sixteenth-century which is presently housed in
the Biblioteca Nacional de Colombia, a surviving artifact after
mass burnings had taken place throughout the Americas. As scholar Cornelius Hegeman highlights in one case:

> It was informed that the bishop Agustin Davila Padilla
> (1599, arrived from Mexico to Santo Domingo) took 300
> copies of the protestant Bible in 1599 and ordered them
> burnt in public. The council of Trent forbade the laity from
> reading the Bible.[7]

Other works were found, such as those of Constantino Ponce de la
Fuente, which had been imported and distributed throughout
Spanish and Portuguese colonies. Once such example is that of
Franciscan bishop Juan de Zumárraga, the first bishop of Mexico,
who applied Ponce's teachings to the Mesoamerican mission field.
In fact, there is evidence that the Nahua and Zacatecas of Mexico
were instructed in the biblical basics of the Christian faith through
Ponce's writings.[8]

On the matter of the converted brothers at the monastery of San
Isidro I will return later, for there are two in particular that I wish to
make mention of. But considering that I had mentioned Constantino
Ponce de la Fuente (1502-1560), it would be fitting that I first address
who he was in the context of everything because he was a significant
influencer and supporter of what went on at the monastery.

---

7. Cornelius Hegeman, *La Reforma en America Latina y el Caribe*
    (Guadalupe, Costa Rica: Editorial CLIR, 2017), 37-38.

8. Andrew L. Wilson, "The Unfortunate Fate of Luther in the
    Ibero-American World" in *Studies in Luther* (USA: Lutheran
    Forum, Summer 2009), 29.

Constantino Ponce de la Fuente

Similar to the case of Julianillo, we do not have an exact date for when Ponce was born. What we do know is that he was born in San Clemente de la Mancha, in the province of Cuenca, and sometime around the year 1502.[9] He appears to have hailed from a Jewish background – however, given his prominence amongst Catholic clergy, he must have been a distant descendant of a Jewish convert. William Jones, in his biography of Ponce, writes that none of Ponce's own books reveal anything of his own ancestry, and the reason for this lies in the anti-Semitic nature of sixteenth-century Spanish culture.[10] Ponce had clearly learned how to conceal certain aspects of himself, something which he would employ when he became a protestant. But before I can address that, I should explain first how he came about his prominence amongst the Catholic clergy, and most especially, amongst the common people of Seville.

Ponce had received a theological education at the Universidad de Alcala, and upon completion of his studies, arrived in Seville in 1533 to carry out his work as a Catholic minister. He was one of two chief preachers at the Sevillan Cathedral, and it is said that many flocked to mass when they learned that it was Ponce who would be preaching. His gift for the exposition of the biblical text can only be grasped through the few writings that have survived to this day. His most notable *Exposition of the First Psalm of David* is a title worth obtaining and reviewing. To quote our dear brother Dr. Ted Van Raalte:

> Ponce delivers God's Word with a beauty and goodness that make its truth not just persuasive, but delightful and won-

---

9. See Maria Paz Aspe Ansa, *Constantino Ponce de la Fuente: El Hombre y su Lenguaje* (Madrid: Universidad Pontificia de Salamanca, 1975), 31.

10. William Jones, *Constantino Ponce de la Fuente* (Nashville, TN.: Vanderbilt University, 1965), 417.

drous. His whole explanation [of Psalm 1], and particularly his contrast of the hearts of the righteous and the wicked, is deeply Reformed.[11]

How did a preacher at the Sevillan Cathedral become prominent amongst the people when what he taught was "Reformed"? The answer is found in that Ponce never publicly declared himself to be Reformed. He knew well than to reveal his cards too soon when the reformation had not yet made significant headway in Spain. He occupied an office, a position, with the privilege of leading the masses down the path of biblical truth, why forfeit this opportunity by mentioning Luther or Calvin when the Scriptural text could speak for itself and therefore save him any needless obstruction? You see, it was around the time that he began his ministerial work in Sevilla that a Spanish protestant reformation movement was just starting to begin. Given his place at the Sevillan Cathedral, Ponce had close fellowship with those of the monastery of San Isidro, and given the later records of the Inquisition, it was not far fetched to assume that many of Ponce's sermons and writings, along with his book collection, were largely due to what had been smuggled into the monastery by Julianillo. But suspicion was not enough to arrest and put to trial such a prominent, well-loved Catholic preacher – not at first. Something more substantive had to have happened, and something did. But prior to that *something*, from 1548 to 1553, Ponce was given the honour of serving as the King's chaplain, and having earned high respect for his moving sermons, his return to Seville may have been with a greater boldness to teach and proclaim the truth recovered by the Reformers. Given the heightened sensitivity, at this point, by the Inquisition, and Ponce's five-year absence, the conditions were ripe for Ponce to be interrogated under suspicion

---

11. Ted Van Raalte, *Endorsement page in The Old Spanish Reformers, Vol. 27: Exposition of the First Psalm of David* (Jordan Station, ON.: Cántaro Publications, 2024).

alone, and he was under investigation until they could attain substantive evidence of his protestant influence. Throughout this time, Ponce confessed his Catholicity, but when he was confronted with a collection of writings from his hand, many of which were explicitly Lutheran, and which had been discovered after having been hidden away in a sympathizer's home, Ponce admitted that what he had written was in fact his profession of faith. He was a covert protestant who had dressed as a Catholic minister, and when he took the pulpit at the Cathedral, he preached unashamedly as a Reformer. Given the favour he had earned from the Spanish king, and how loved he was by the people, Ponce was offered a chance to recant. Ponce refused. It is said that when King Charles V, whom Ponce had served as chaplain, discovered Ponce's sentencing as a protestant heretic, he exclaimed in disappointment: "You could not have condemned a greater man… if Constantino is a heretic, he is a great one."[12] There was, of course, no changing the course for the Spanish King, who was also considered the Holy Roman Emperor, in terms of his civil authority.

Ponce, like many others, died a martyr's death, but in Ponce's case, he did not make it as far as to a public execution. While awaiting the date of his execution, it is said that he suffered dysentery while imprisoned at the Castle of Triana, and died of natural causes. Those who despised him began to invent stories of his death, claiming that he had committed suicide and therefore damned his soul to hell, but as the twentieth-century scholar P. A. Rodriguez writes, "These Romanist accounts, far from being consistent, decisively contradict each other."[13] Ponce died unashamedly for the faith he had in

---

12. Cited in J. MacPherson, "The Reformation in Spain: Its Suppression."

13. P. A. Rodriguez, "Preliminary Notice", in *The Old Spanish Reformers,* Vol. 27: The Exposition of the First Psalm of David (Jordan Station, ON.: Cántaro Publications, 2024), xxiii.

the biblical gospel, and in stark opposition to the corruption and false teaching of the Roman Catholic Church.

C. de Reina and C. de Valera

There are two more figures I wish to call our attention to, Casiodoro de Reina (1520-1594) and Cipriano de Valera (1531-1602), both of whom were monks at the monastery of San Isidro del Campo. I will begin first with Reina, because it is believed that he served as a mentor for a time for Valera.

Reina is believed to have been born in the year 1520 in Montemolin, in the province of Badajoz. His early interest in the Christian Scriptures led to him becoming a monk of the Hieronymite monastery in 1557. It is believed that during his service as a monk, he would not only have known Ponce but also have benefited from his teachings and mentorship. His time at the monastery, however, was short-lived. At some point, he became a protestant after having read the protestant works that had been smuggled into the monastery. And instead of simply being an observant and quiet protestant convert, he became a central figure in the growth and organization of the protestants in Seville. Some say that he may have occupied an informal pastoral role over those who had come to faith.[14] Whatever that might have looked like, it did not last long, because the Inquisition had caught whiff of what had been transpiring at the monastery of San Isidro. Not all the monks were protestants, but a significant number were. Having been tipped off that the Inquisition was soon to fall upon the monastery, several protestant converts fled from Spain. Reina and Valera were amongst those who fled. Where would

---

14. See Gordon A. Kinder, *Casiodoro de Reina: Spanish Reformer of the Sixteenth Century* (London, UK.: Tamesis Books Limited, 1975); Andres Messmer, *Casiodoro de Reina: Su vida, Biblia y teología: Ensayos en honor del 500 aniversario de su nacimiento* (Madrid: Editorial CLIE, 2023).

they go? Each Spanish reformer has their own story. In Reina's case, he traveled to Geneva with Valera in 1558. But with news that a friend of his had been killed, that being the Unitarian heretic Servetus, Reina feared that Geneva was becoming a "new Rome." This led to Reina migrating from Geneva to London, England. By this time, which was the year 1559, England had opened its borders to protestant refugees. Prior to this, there was a terrible persecution of protestants under Queen Mary I, which had lasted from the year 1553 to 1558. But now, under Elizabethan rule, England was becoming a refuge for protestant foreigners. This was where Reina would first settle, and this was where Reina would plant a church for Spanish-speaking protestants. This was also where he would write and publish, with Valera's editorial assistance, *The Spanish Confession of the Christian Faith*. And furthermore, this is where Reina would begin to dedicate more time towards realizing his dream, the complete Spanish translation of the Old and New Testaments.

To keep the story short, after a few years, Reina would be forced to flee England, finding a home in Frankfurt. The Inquisition had been keeping tabs of his progress, of the church he planted, of the Spanish Confession he had written for the Consistory of churches in London – which no doubt Reina would have sent a copy to the King of Spain – and they were particularly wary of his work on translating the entire Bible into Spanish. So, in an effort to dislodge him from the safe harbours of England, the Inquisition bribed a fellow Spanish exile to construct a scandal and falsely accuse Reina. It worked, in the sense that Reina was frightened and fled for his life, though it would become clear after several legal proceedings that the accuser had been offered safe return to Spain if he could sabotage Reina's character and ministry. The accusations were proven to be false, but it had done its damage. It was 1564 when Reina arrived in Frankfurt, and by God's grace he evaded the Inquisition, while enroute through Antwerp, who had its agents searching for him throughout Europe. Having settled there with his family, he dedicated most of his time towards completing his Spanish translation of the Bible. And when it was completed, it was published in 1569 as *La Biblia del Oso*, named after a bear because of its front cover imagery, and likely having to do also with the name of the printer.

Looking back, Reina's translation was no small feat. He had used a number of ancient texts that were available at his disposal to realize his translation, including the Ferrara Bible (Hebrew Bible) in Ladino, the Masoretic text, the Vetus Latina, the Receptus of Erasmus, and even various Syriac manuscripts. And he was not without assistance, Pérez de Pineda's earlier New Testament translation aided Reina in the full text edition that he was working on. It is thanks to his work that Spanish-speakers all around the world today have the Reina-Valera Bible translation.

Now, having mentioned the Reina-Valera Bible translation – the reason that Valera's name is tacked on there is because Valera also had a significant contribution. And he will be the last figure that I have time to highlight this morning.

Cipriano de Valera (1531-1602), born in Fregenal de la Sierra, north of Seville, was a student for six years at the University of Seville. And while there he studied Dialectics and Philosophy, graduating with a bachelor's degree. In his early twenties, presumably after his studies, he became a member of the Order of Observantine Hieronymites, and there served at the monastery of San Isidro alongside Reina and other protestants (there were probably about twenty monks that were covert protestants). Unlike those who remained behind and were martyred in a most brutal fashion by the Inquisition, Valera managed to escape with Reina and found his place of refuge first in Geneva. Now, while Reina was quick to flee to England due to his friendship with Servetus, it is believed that Valera stayed longer. Over the course of time, Reina would become less Calvinistic in his theology and more Lutheran, eventually writing a Lutheran catechism towards the latter years of his life, but the same could not be said of Valera. Valera was very much an image of Calvin in his thinking and theology, which is due in large part to the fact that he single-handedly translated Calvin's *Institutes of the Christian Religion* into Spanish. Valera did not, however, stay in Geneva long-term. Given how many heretics had come out from the land of Spain, and by this I mean heretics as regarded by both Catholics and protestants alike, there was a particular disdain in Geneva against the Spanish. And feeling unwelcome, Valera followed Reina's path to England. However, as opposed to settling in London, as Reina did, he went on to take a position at the University of Cambridge as Professor of Theology, eventually becoming a Fellow of Magdalene College. And in the year 1565, he received his Master's degree from the University of Oxford, a testament to his intellectual vigor and sharpness of doctrine. He would become known, to the chagrin of the Inquisition, as the Spanish reformer *par excellence*.[15]

Now, from between this time of his academic achievements to his later move to London, we have little historical information, but what we do know is that protestant England considered Valera to be a most valuable asset in its conflict with Catholic Spain. Several works were written by Valera while in England, such as *Los Dos Tratados del Papa y la Misa* and *Un Tratado para confirmar en la fe Cristiana a los cautivos de Berberia*, which were considered theological, Reformed artillery since they were printed and disseminated into Spanish territories after the failed invasion of the Spanish Armada.[16]

It is fair to say that we know more of Valera's achievements and his writings than of his personal life at this point, thus far at least, but what

---

15. See Steven R. Martins, "Cipriano de Valera: Spanish Reformer par excellence" in *La Fuente: Iberoamerican Journal for Christian Worldview*, Vol. 4, No. 1, 2024.

16. Ibid.

we do know occurred *after* this period of his life was that, after Reina had fled the country due to the scandal orchestrated by the Inquisition, he moved to London to take on the pastoral mantle of the Spanish church that had been started there. What happened to that church is still a question historians have yet to answer, but it may just be that Valera was its second and final pastor. All of this gives you a bit of an idea as to the life of Valera, and what he contributed, but perhaps the most significant contribution was his editorial work on Reina's Spanish Bible translation. And this is in fact the last historical note we have on record of his life. In 1602, the second edition of Reina's Bible translation was published as *La Biblia del Cántaro*. Valera didn't touch much of Reina's translation work, but he did re-organize its content to better reflect the structure of other translated protestant Bibles. This included the omission of the apocrypha and the grouping of Old and New Testament books into how they are reflected in our Bibles today. This was considered his life's final achievement, his *magnum opus*, and he was most happy to do this in service to the Lord, and in love for every person who spoke the Spanish tongue.[17]

Well, four historical figures, and we have only scratched the surface of the Spanish Reformation. Unfortunately, I do not have time to delve deeper. Let me, however, highlight a few resources for your own reading and consideration, and then proceed to what we can learn for today.

Writings, Archived Works, and Future Publications

For those interested in learning more about the Spanish Reformation, there are several writings and archived works worth surveying. There is, for example, that monumental collection published in the mid-nineteenth century by the Spaniard Luis de Usoz y Rio, with the limited help of the Englishman Benjamin Baron Wiffen. This collection was a twenty-volume compilation of writings of the Spanish reformers, pub-

17. Ibid.

lished solely in Spanish as *Reformistas Antiguos Españoles* (1847-1865). It is a work that the Cántaro Institute has committed to not only translate into English but expand with other works that were excluded, likely due to Usoz y Rio's lack of access to other manuscripts at the time. One such publication of the *Old Spanish Reformers* that is now in print today is Ponce's *Exposition of the First Psalm of David*, dated to about 1546. We have almost near to completion Vol. 31, which is Juan de Valdés' *Dialogue of Doctrine*, and Vol. 24, which is a collection of Valdés' *Short Treatises*, as well as Cipriano de Valera's own writings.

Other titles worth considering are the *Bibliotheca Wiffeniana*, which is a three-volume set; Marcel Bataillon's two-volume set *Erasme et l'Espagne*, Paul J. Hauben's *Three Spanish Heretics*, Casiodoro de Reina's *Spanish Confession of the Christian Faith*, and a recent re-typeset by the Cántaro Institute, the *History of the Spanish Reformation* by Thomas M'Crie. There are certainly several other works to consult, and these are but a few, but our hope in the coming years is to be able to bring much more of this material into the common English tongue in order that the church today might benefit from what wisdom the Spanish reformers have to offer us.

Concluding Remarks

Now, last but not least, I wish to make a few short remarks on what we can draw from the Spanish reformation, particularly what I have addressed this morning, for our living *Coram Deo*, before the face of God. The first of these remarks is concerning the power of the Word of God, and its necessity for its clear presentation.

The Power of Scripture in the Common Tongue

When we look back at the efforts of the humble *Julianillo*, for example, in smuggling Spanish Scriptures and Reformed literature into a hostile culture, and as we discover the transformation this began to bring about in the hearts of those who read them, we're reminded of the transformative power of the Word of God, and the necessity of having that inspired Word accessible in our own tongue. We have no shortage of Bibles in English and Spanish, but we can probably think of various people groups around the world who still do not have a full Bible translation in their mother tongue. If you were to travel to Washington, DC, and pay a visit to the Museum of the Bible, there is an exhibit there with a vast library of books, and each book has the word "Bible" written on it but in different languages. And those books represent Bibles that have yet to be translated into whatever language is on that book cover. It may be difficult to imagine given our rich protestant heritage today, but just two years ago, to cite an example, the Old Testament was fully translated for the first time in the Eastern Apurimac Quechua language of Peru.[18] There is a need to support more Bible translations so that all may hear and know the truth of God and the gospel revealed therein.

Furthermore, as it relates to Julianillo's devotion to the Lord, and his passionate dedication to his mission – for in this sense he really was a missionary – we ought to feel exhorted to seek to make the Scriptures clear and comprehensible to all. Not all of us can participate meaningfully in translating the Word into another tongue, but all of us can certainly seek to translate its message into a language that the common person today can understand. There is a significant gulf of understanding between today's generation and when the Scriptures were written. Who else but the church of Christ can interpret and explain these Scriptures to the people? Like Philip with the Eunuch in Acts 8:26-40, we are called to explain the Scriptures, to

---

18. "Quechua translators reach Bible translation milestone", *Wycliffe Canada*. Accessed November 12, 2024, https://www.wycliffe.ca/quechua-translators-reach-bible-translation-milestone/.

sow the seed of the gospel, trusting that the Lord will do His work of salvation and renewal. Is that something that we can set our hearts to do? Whatever may be our eschatological position, one thing that we can all agree on is our mission as God's church for the here and now.

Faithfulness in Adversity

My second remark draws from what God did through figures like Julianillo and Constantino Ponce de la Fuente. These men withstood terrible punishments, they were publicly condemned and slandered, humiliated before the eyes of all men, and yet their spirits never broke. Was there some strength in their spirits which they could call their own? No, not at all. The strength of spirit we see in both Julianillo and Ponce was of the Holy Spirit, for how else can we account for their unshakable conviction and perseverance in the face of such suffering and death? They were martyrs, whether they died burned at the stake or died in the dungeon of the Castillo de Triana. And such sacrifice is worthy of our attention, for they remind us of the courage we must have to be bold witnesses in a hostile culture, and that such courage can only be mustered when we are wholly dependent on the Spirit of God. Our times may be quite different, the enemies of God may look quite different, but our missional context remains much the same in the sense that we are God's people, in a fallen, hostile world, and we are called to proclaim the truth, anticipating both positive reaction to the gospel, as well as negative hostility and persecution. In such times where we must wrestle with our culture's increasing apostasy, with the on-going moral and sexual revolutions, and the rise and dissemination of false philosophies of life, cultural Marxism not excluded, we must be willing and able to proclaim the true philosophy of life, the Christian worldview we all embrace and confess, the inspired, inscripturated revelation of God, and the Christ it reveals and exalts.

Semper Reformanda

Lastly, drawing from figures such as Reina and Valera, who translated and refined the Spanish Bible, we can discern in them the spirit of *Semper Reformanda*, the church always reforming according to Scripture. Is that spirit prevalent amongst God's church today? Are we continually seeking to be reformed to the clear teaching of Scripture? And I do not just mean in terms of our ecclesiology, for many think this applies to the institutional church and nothing more, no, I mean everything we do in every sphere of life, in utter defiance of the false sacred-secular divide upheld by our culture. It was the American Christian philosopher H. Evan Runner who said that "Life is Religion", and in the sense that everything we do is an act of worship, and driven by a religious heart-commitment, he is absolutely right. All of life must be lived for all of Christ, for otherwise, our lives are either oriented in an apostate direction, or compromised by some synthesis of truth and error. As God's people, living *Coram Deo*, before the face of God, we must seek to do all things in such a way that honours and glorifies our God. And to do so, we must embrace that reformational spirit, to reform our hearts and minds to the will of God revealed and expressed in His inspired Word. Christ is Lord, and our lives ought to reflect that He is Lord over all.

With that I close. And may we prepare our hearts and minds for Dr. Ted Van Raalte's next talk on "The Reformation in Europe."

The Reformation in Europe:
God's Gracious Gift,
A Truly Catholic Reformation

DR. THEODORE G. VAN RAALTE

Introduction

FROM THE EARLY TO the middle and into the latter stages of the Reformation, diverse Christian figures were united by a common purpose. They sought to correct the prevalent errors of the Roman Catholic Church throughout Europe by returning to the Word of God.

I would like to speak about the Reformation in Europe, and I want the initial focus to be on the Catholicity of the Reformation—we have diverse places, diverse people, diverse languages, and yet there was unity as they all sought reform in accordance with the Word of God. Whether among the Spanish, English, German, French, or Dutch, there was a wonderful unity in diversity, a oneness in faith. We worship our glorious Lord God Almighty when we see this.

Reform took root at nearly the same time in each of the areas of Europe, whether German-speaking or French-speaking in the Swiss areas, and whether these Christians of Europe were French, German, English, Italian, Spanish, or Dutch. The common impetus was the Word of God, which the Spirit used in each place.

I have here a map of Europe that illustrates the international diversity which characterized the Reformation.[1] The map, which highlights Spain, Italy, France, the Netherlands, Lowlands, England, Scotland, and Ireland, is coloured to show whether the areas were more Roman Catholic, Lutheran, or Reformed.

To offer context to the Reformed period in Europe, let's notice that a variety of Pre-Reformation figures had already publicly prompted reform in the existing Roman Catholic Church. The Lord used them to prepare much of Europe in the late fifteenth and early sixteenth centuries, prior to the Reformation. The Waldensians, for example, pursued reformation in southern France, while Girolamo Savonarola led moral reform in the north of Italy (in Florence). John Huss saw reformation in present-day Czechoslovakia, while Erasmus of Rotterdam impacted the Reformation everywhere by his work on the Greek text of the New Testament and his criticism of the Roman clergy. Jacques Lefèvre contributed to the reformation in France, and Wyclif laid foundations for it in England. The geographic locations of these pre-Reformation figures were diverse. Yet, independent from one another, each figure displayed a strong impetus for reform, whether it be mostly moral reform or doctrinal reform.

We see a similar situation with the reformers. Luther and Melanchthon were in Germany; Zwingli and Bullinger were in Zurich; Bucer was in Strasbourg; Farel and Calvin were in Geneva and other towns like Neuchâtel and Lausanne. In England, we know of Cranmer; in Scotland, Knox and Melville. In Spain, Constantino Ponce de la Fuente preached reformation doctrines though he remained in the Roman Church. Peter Martyr Vermigli and Jerome Zanchi both had to leave Italy to save their lives. They then helped the Reformation in Strasbourg and in England, where they preached and taught

---

1. See maps in the appendix.

men to become pastors. In the French-speaking areas we have Guido de Brès and Antoine de Chandieu, whom we will soon discuss.

The point of the matter is this—these figures were situated all over Europe. It was not as though one person sent a letter out to all these people in Europe, insisting, "O, let's start a reformation." God's Word and Spirit were already working in each of these locations, and as God's Word came to be understood by these reformers, they said in agreement, "We need to live by grace, and by His Word, for we have come to understand it rightly." They said, "We need to live by grace. We need to worship God for His glory, and we have to stop having this sort of meritocratic thing where we're earning our way with God. It is all by grace." The Word of God was discovered in each place around the same time. Of course, they influenced each other to some degree, but in very significant ways, God's Spirit remarkably motivated and moved people in different places towards reformation. The Catholicity of the Reformation also grew out of the reality that reform was needed in each place due to the widespread false teachings and unhealthy spiritual practices that had developed within the Roman Church.[2] Prior to the Reformation, there was an increase in emotionalism, money-making, superstition, and indulgences. During the mid-to-late 1400s, the consecrated host was the center of all worship—it is the actual body and blood of Christ! They said—and it was claimed to be made hundreds of times per day upon the hundreds of altars in each cathedral. The high moment of saying the Mass was the ringing of the bell, which occurred when the priest finished saying in Latin, *"Hoc est corpus meum"* ("This is my body"). At that moment, all the worshippers must bow or at least genuflect. This happened hundreds of times a day, occa-

---

2. See sidebar in the appendix.

sionally at the same time on different altars within some of these large church buildings.

The leftover consecrated hosts were traditionally kept in sacred containers called tabernacles, designed to house the Eucharist with reverence and care. These tabernacles were often ornate, emphasizing the sacredness of their contents. Additionally, consecrated hosts were sometimes placed in gilded monstrances—elaborate vessels, often adorned with gold and jewels, specifically crafted to display the Eucharist for adoration and public processions.

These practices, which date back to the medieval and Renaissance periods, continue in the Roman Catholic Church today. Modern tabernacles and monstrances still serve as focal points for worship, just as they did centuries ago. If you visit a museum or a Roman Catholic church, you can often find historical examples of these gilded objects, reflecting the enduring tradition of reverence for the consecrated host.

What, then, do I want to say about looking at the Reformation in Europe? And why did I show you the map with names and all these different places, arising around the same time (see appendix)?

There is one God, there is one Christ, and there is one humanity. And we all have basically the same kind of heart. And so, there is one gospel, one saving word for all people—this has remained unchanged throughout the ages. People have adulterated it and messed it up and not taught it correctly. But when it is rediscovered, it is the same in every place and time, and it is needed in the same way always. This is what I want you all to have a feel for and to know—the Catholicity, then, of the Reformation.

Now, the progress of the Reformation went through stages. Therefore, I will represent its progress, in the 1500s, through three French-speaking Reformed figures from the early, mid, and later Reformation:

- Early Reformation: Guillaume Farel (1489–1565)
- Middle Reformation: Guido de Brès (1522–1567)
- Later Reformation: Antoine de Chandieu (1534–1591)

Early Reformation: Guillaume Farel (1489–1565)

Guillaume Farel studied in Paris and received his Master of Arts at the age of 28. Under the mentorship of Jacques Lefèvre d'Étaples, a pre-Reformation figure, Farel was influenced by reform-minded thought that sought renewal within the Roman Catholic Church. This intellectual foundation laid the groundwork for Farel's later pivotal role in advancing the Reformation, particularly in securing John Calvin for Geneva.

Between 1521 and 1523, Farel worked under Bishop Guillaume Briçonnet, a reform-minded bishop in the town of Meaux (about 50 km East of Paris). Briçonnet, desiring to see the gospel preached in Meaux, discovered that most of his clergy were ill-equipped for this task—out of 100 clergy, only 14 were capable of preaching the gospel, and 43 could not rightly administer the sacraments. After giving 60 clergy members a year to improve, most were ultimately dismissed. This experience revealed the desperate need for reform and helped shape Farel's commitment to the proclamation of the gospel and the Reformation's broader mission. This was the beginning, then, of Farel's gospel preaching—he was not really ordained as such, but Briçonnet's orders gave him a license to preach. This is where he began to learn the practice of preaching.

Learning Prayer as You Pray

By 1524, Farel, having himself grown up in a Roman Catholic context, observed that people were constantly praying the Lord's Prayer in Latin, which was incomprehensible to the common person. He sought to reform this practice by encouraging prayer in French so that people could understand it. Farel thus wrote a treatise called "Le

Guillaume Farel (1489–1565)

Paternoster" (the Our Father), which he wrote in French as a prayer from beginning to end, spanning about twenty-five pages in length.[3]

Remarkably, Farel sought to teach prayer by way of praying. Instead of instructing people with abstract concepts, he wrote a prayer based on the Lord's Prayer that taught its meaning as one prayed through it. His goal was not only to teach meaningful prayer but also to inflame the heart—personal religious experience does matter. New riches had been discovered and needed to be shared.

One of the baptism prayers commonly used in Reformed churches today contains significant echoes of Farel's prayer from the first Reformed liturgy in the French language. This demonstrates how the practices introduced during the Reformation continue to shape and unite Reformed worship across diverse contexts.

Farel's prayer approach was meant to replace the Roman Catholic *Book of Hours*,[4] which prescribed set prayers for various hours of the day, and suggested prayers to various saints for specific needs (e.g., finding lost items or directions). Instead, Farel emphasized the Lord's Prayer, teaching believers to engage their hearts and minds in meaningful prayer rooted in Scripture. Through this, doctrine is

---

3.   This prayer is available in English translation in, Jason Zuidema and Theodore Van Raalte, *Early French Reform: The Theology and Spirituality of Guillaume Farel* (Farnham, Surrey: Ashgate, 2011), 105–116.

4.   The *Book of Hours* is a medieval devotional book used primarily by lay Christians, structured around prayers and psalms for specific hours of the day, often richly illustrated and reflecting the liturgical calendar. While serving as a tool for personal piety, it became a symbol of rote religiosity and superstition, as its use often prioritized ritual over genuine faith. Guillaume Farel's *La Paternoster* critiques the *Book of Hours* for promoting mechanical prayer and neglecting the centrality of heartfelt devotion to God, redirecting attention to Christ as the true mediator rather than ritualistic practices. See Zuidema and Van Raalte, *Early French Reform*, 50–55.

learned and internalized as one prays, transforming both worship and personal devotion.

Thirteen Theses in Latin

In 1524, Farel was compelled to cease teaching and preaching in Meaux due to opposition from a cleric who ranked higher than Briçonnet. Farel thus relocated to Basel, where Erasmus resided. It was one of the centers for reform efforts. Farel attempted to secure the approval of Basel's city council for a public disputation wherein he would argue for further reformation. On March 3, 1524, Farel posted 13 theses in Latin to be publicly argued. However, a disagreement between the university and the bishop prevented the disputation, highlighting the institutional challenges faced by reformers. The bishop opposed Farel, demanding his removal from the city.

However, the university expressed an interest in hearing both sides, and the city magistrates, favoring reform, ordered the disputation to proceed. They further mandated that all citizens, especially clergy, must attend, demonstrating how Reformation ideas were being debated not only within ecclesiastical circles but also in civic and academic contexts.

In his fourth thesis, Farel critiqued the memorial mass, or prayers for the dead, a practice funded by the laity and carried out by chantry[5] priests through low masses. He argued:

---

5. [Editor's Note:] Endowed chantries in Roman Catholicism refer to specific types of ecclesiastical endowments or foundations established to fund the celebration of Masses, particularly for the soul of the person who provided the endowment or their family members. The term "chantry" comes from the Old French word chanterie, meaning "singing," as these foundations were often associated with choral Masses or prayers for the dead. See Zuidema and Van Raalte, *Early French Reform*, 41.

> Long-winded prayers which are against the command of
> Christ and not according to Christian patterns cannot
> be prayed or instituted without danger. Thus, it will be
> better to pay out to the poor whatever is offered in these
> matters, and not to contribute to the funding of so
> many evils.[6]

These chantries, which rose in prominence during the 15th and early 16th centuries, often involved paying priests to perform extra masses or funding the construction of alcoves or altars in church buildings, wherein these memorial masses for the dead could be observed. Farel's critique highlights a shared Reformation principle: rejecting practices that encouraged financial exploitation and thus used up money that the poor needed. At the same time the chantries embellished and tarnished the true worship of God. There was a universal need for reform.

Some cathedrals across Europe feature additional structures on their sides—chantries funded by laity who also paid priests to say masses for deceased loved ones, often to reduce their time in purgatory. While such financial giving may have seemed pious and loving, reformers like Farrel critiqued them as practices that distracted from true worship and biblical doctrine. This critique was part of a shared Reformation effort to address such widespread abuses and return the church to the authority of Scripture.

Between 1515 and 1518, the diocese around Geneva counted some 1,435 endowed chantries, with the Cathedral of Saint Pierre alone housing 100 chantries and 23 altars by 1536.[7] This was not unique to Geneva; such practices were widespread across Europe. Legal requirements for founding a chantry—such as the need to provide funds for both its setup and ongoing maintenance—of-

---

6. Zuidema and Van Raalte, *Early French Reform*, 40.

7. Zuidema and Van Raalte, *Early French Reform*, 40–41.

ten denied the poor much-needed resources. Farel and other reformers critiqued this as a significant abuse, part of their shared commitment to aligning church practices with Scripture and prioritizing care for the poor.

Farel, in fact, expanded on this critique five years later in his *Summa*, a summary of doctrine, where he argued that the mass impoverished the poor, widows, and orphans. By it, he stressed, "the church of the pope gains all the goods of the world, leaving the poor destitute."[8] In 1545, sixteen years later, Farel expanded a prayer for confessing sins that he had first written in 1543, lengthening it by over 100 pages. These heartfelt prayers, which praise the Father, the Son, and the Holy Spirit, and then return to the Son and then to the Father, have a deeply Trinitarian structure.

What did he say in this prayer of 1545 about confessing sins? He said, "What a great number of foundations! And all this is done from the substance of the poor widows, orphans, and the blood of the poor people! All this cries out for and demands vengeance upon us."[9] He exposes the superstitious thinking—as if we are going to help our grandmother get out of purgatory, while the people around us are dying.

A Bold and Pastoral Itinerant Preacher

In 1528, the City Council of Bern, one of the powerful Swiss cantons, commissioned Farel to preach in Swiss towns, assuring him that if anyone harmed him, they would have to answer to the city of Bern. Farel's itinerant preaching earned him the title "Apostle of the Alps," reflecting his pastoral boldness and dedication to spreading the Gospel even under opposition. Like medieval missionaries, who were known as apostles to specific regions (e.g., Willibrord, apostle to the Frisians), Farel, known as the "Apostle of the Alps," often faced

---

8. Zuidema and Van Raalte, *Early French Reform*, 41, 136.

9. Ibid., 41.

fierce opposition when preaching.[10] In one town, after being expelled from the church building by the local priest or custodian—as sometimes happened with the aid of soldiers—he continued his ministry undeterred, preaching in the cemetery beside the church. Opponents then rang the church bell to drown out Farel's preaching, but his powerful voice rose above the noise, allowing him to proclaim the Gospel clearly. Such boldness in his itinerant preaching earned him the title "Apostle of the Alps." I examined his travels, as reported in an excellent scholarly biography of Farel from 1930, and it turns out that over the span of 44 years in the Swiss Alps, Farel spent time in approximately 165 destinations. These were 165 places where he stayed for at least a week or two to preach the gospel, catechize people, and teach them how to pray.[11] Of course, he worked in some for years.

Farel was also responsible for the first Reformed confession in French in 1530, the *Summaire*, and the first Reformed liturgy in French in 1533. With the ongoing support of the city of Bern, Farel came to Geneva, and urged the City Council to follow the example of other Swiss cantons around them, such as Zurich, where Zwingli led the Reformation, and Basel, which had embraced evangelical teaching. However, Geneva rudely expelled him, resisting his call for reform.

In 1529, Farel was expelled from Geneva, and again in 1532, despite having a letter of protection from the city of Bern. He preached openly at the end of 1533 and engaged in public debates with Guy Furbity in 1534 and Pierre Caroli in 1535, and in August 1535, Geneva abolished the mass through a decision by the City

10. Theodore G. Van Raalte, "Apostle of the Alps: Guillaume Farel and the Reforming of Geneva," in *Brill Companion to the Reformation in Geneva*, ed. Jon Balserak (Leiden: Brill, 2021), 51–3.

11. Comité Farel, *Guillaume Farel: 1489–1565: Biographie Nouvelle* (Neuchâtel: 1930), 745–6.

Council.[12] It is important to understand that this reflects the close relationship between church and state at the time, rather than a modern notion of their separation.

In May 1536, the city voted for full reform according to the Gospel. By January 1537, Geneva had adopted a new confession of faith and new articles governing religion. These changes were decided by citizen votes, making them public events and part of a great cultural movement. While these developments in 1536 and 1537 were very positive, tensions also arose. In 1538, Farel, Calvin—who had joined in 1536— and an older preacher named Courauld were expelled from Geneva because they refused to administer the Lord's Supper.[13]

The preachers believed that confessing faith and swearing to the confession were proper prerequisites for coming to the Lord's table. Since the city refused to require all citizens to swear to the confession, the preachers refused to administer the Lord's Supper. A synod in Zurich later admonished the pastors, advising them to be less demanding and to continue patient preaching.

Preaching the Gospel at every opportunity
Although Farel never again served as a pastor in Geneva after 1538, he used his influence to support Calvin's return there in 1541. Farel remained in close contact with Calvin and occasionally preached in Geneva. Over time, Geneva became a 'city on a hill,' attracting reformers like John Knox, who trained there before bringing the Reformation to Scotland.

I want to give you a glimpse into what it was like to be someone like Farel or Calvin at the time. For Calvin, his preaching schedule was relentless—seven days on, meaning he preached every single day of the week, early in the morning, and then on Sundays fulfilled the additional duties required for that day. This was also the routine in

---

12. Van Raalte, "Apostle of the Alps," 63–8.

13. Van Raalte, "Apostle of the Alps," 69–70.

Neuchâtel, another Swiss town, where Farel pastored for decades. Farel preached four sermons each Sunday, sometimes presenting one for the servants early in the morning and repeating it for the rest of the congregation later. He also preached three sermons on weekdays, totaling seven sermons per week—about 350 per year and possibly over 12,000 in his lifetime. His tireless efforts highlight the central role of preaching in the Reformation.

This is the way of the Reformation—you need preachers who are relentlessly busy, preaching the Gospel at every opportunity.

One of the ways you may know Farel is the same way I first learned about him. I remember a church history textbook from my time in Christian school showing Farel standing up, shaking his finger, and fiercely admonishing Calvin, who was cowering before him, saying, "If in this hour of Geneva's need, you leave Geneva, God curse your studies." It is something of an urban myth to know Farel only as the fiery preacher shaking his finger at Calvin. But it is true that in 1536, when Calvin was passing through Geneva on his way to another city, Farel persuaded him to stay because he was deeply committed to securing preachers for the Reformation cause—by 1536, he had already managed to secure around 40 gospel preachers.[14] One famous example is Pierre Viret, secured by Farel. If you think these actions of Farel toward Calvin were unusual, consider Calvin's own account of these events in his preface to his commentary on the Psalms, for, when you turn the page, you discover that in 1538, after Calvin was expelled from Geneva and went to Strasbourg, Bucer remonstrated with him in the same way Farel had in 1536, calling on God to insist that Calvin remain in Strasbourg and serve there.[15]

---

14. Zuidema and Van Raalte, *Early French Reform*, 99.
15. Van Raalte, "Apostle of the Alps," 68–9.

It is important to remember that Farel and Calvin were not formally ordained. You may have seen a pastor ordained in our era, with hands laid on him as a symbol of prayer for the Holy Spirit. Farel and Calvin, however, lived in a time of transition when the Reformed churches had not yet fully organized such practices. And so, these men sometimes felt the need to justify the lawfulness of their ministry. For example, when Farel was called upon to preach and the hearers also needed the sacraments, he asked Oecolampadius whether he ought to do so. Oecolampadius was a reformer in Basel who had already been ordained in the Roman church prior to the Reformation. Oecolampadius told him that he would need to administer the sacraments as well. Similarly, when a nobleman asked him to come and preach in his castle, he went. Farel would later refer back to this request, as well as Oecolampadius's advice, in ways that make me think that he regarded these to be grounds for his ministerial calling.[16]

Farel made several contributions unique to the Swiss Reformation among French speakers. Readers of his letters and published works, many of which were prayers, cannot miss the spiritual depth of Farel. He was, in many ways, a man of all heart—full of concern for others to know the Gospel, passionate in preaching, and lofty in prayer. His published prayers and his preservation of the ancient phrase, "Let us lift up our hearts to the Lord," from the early church, carried this tradition forward into Reformed worship, leaving a lasting legacy.[17]

Farel's fundamental concern was to inflame hearts rather than promote rote learning. This reflects theology in action, emphasizing the side of the Reformation that engaged the affections as well as the

---

16. Zuidema and Van Raalte, *Early French Reform*, 26, 47n 68.

17. Van Raalte, "Apostle of the Alps," 72.

mind. He was also a skilled organizer, as seen in his efforts to recruit many preachers.

All these men in the early Reformation were deeply committed to preaching, burdened with a spiritual desire to reach the common people for their salvation. Their hearts burned with the need to share the way to a new and living relationship with the Lord. These first-generation reformers also utilized the prior training they had received in institutions controlled by the Roman Catholic Church.

When new students for the ministry came, they could still rely on foundational teachings—such as the doctrine of the Trinity, the two natures of Christ, and the ancient creeds—learned in other institutions. Then, they could come and listen to the daily preaching happening in Geneva, Zurich, Strasbourg, Basel, and other Reformation centers.

Farel's ministry is, in a sense, uncomplicated—heartfelt and responsive to the needs of the hour, always keeping the main thing, the main thing. He focused on teaching the Lord's Prayer and the Creed in French, making the Gospel accessible to the people. He was truly a man of the first hour.

After the first generation of Reformers, such as Farel, God raised up other figures in accordance with his providential purposes. He grounded each one in gospel truth, maintaining the catholicity of the Reformation. God brought about reform in Europe through diverse figures in accordance with His providential purposes, leading us to discuss our next person.

Middle Reformation: Guido de Brès (1522–1567)

Early Years and Academic Pilgrimage
Let us now consider Guido de Brès, who was born in 1522 in what is now southern Belgium. At the time of his birth, John Calvin was just thirteen years old, and five years had passed since Luther nailed his 95 Theses to the church door in Wittenberg. Though little is

Guido de Brès (1522–1567)

known about his childhood, while he was in the womb, his mother deeply desired that her child would be a son who would preach the Gospel. At the time, she might have said a son who would say Mass, but God had greater plans. De Brès received part of his education in England and part in Lausanne and Geneva, traveling to these cities to obtain the best theological education available.

In his late twenties, de Brès, already reform-minded, traveled to England and joined the Congregation of Refugees. Ministers trained in the 16th century often undertook what could be called an academic pilgrimage, moving between centers of theological education. They might study in Heidelberg, spend six months in Geneva, and later go to Leiden or Lausanne.

After 1575, they could also train in Leiden's newly established university. Such "academic pilgrimages" reflect the catholicity of the Reformation, as ministers were trained in diverse places yet received the same Gospel-centered education. Whether in Lausanne, Cambridge, Heidelberg, or Scotland, the focus remained consistent. Brès learned much in England and Lausanne and likely in Geneva, though Geneva's academy didn't begin until 1559. Lausanne's theological academy provided earlier opportunities.

The Belgian Confession

Guido de Brès chose not to remain in England but to return to the French-speaking Lowlands of Belgium, driven by his love for Christ and his fellow believers. There, he ministered to persecuted (French-speaking) churches, putting himself at great risk. To evade capture, he never stayed in one place for long, frequently changing his name, altering his appearance by growing or trimming his beard, and varying his clothing. He took great measures to avoid capture, contributing to the Reformation through numerous publications, though his name appears on just one. His wife, Catherine Ramon, displayed immense courage by marrying him during his perilous ministry, when they had no permanent home. He was then 38 years old. By the time Guido was martyred seven years later, God had blessed them with five children. Amidst this backdrop, Brès completed the Belgian Confession in 1561, a foundational document for Reformed believers, crafted in strict secrecy.[18]

The Belgic Confession, with its scriptural richness and beauty, was quickly adopted by many Reformed churches in the years following its creation.[19] The Belgian Confession of 1561

---

18. Wes Bredenhof, *For the Cause of the Son of God: The Missiological Significance of the Belgic Confession* (Reformation Media and Press, 2011).

19. Nicolaas H. Gootjes, *The Belgic Confession: Its History and Sources* (Baker: Grand Rapids, MI, 2008), 93–115. Dr. Gootjes was my professor of dogmatics. His dedication to unraveling historical mysteries and solving theological questions through meticulous research is evident in this work.

was heavily influenced by the French Confession of 1559, and recent scholarship has expanded on what Dr. N. H.Gootjes initially uncovered. Moreover, the French Confession itself traces back to a 1557 letter to the king, demonstrating the layered history and international dialogue of Reformation theology. The big question is, who wrote that letter to the king in 1557? It was likely Antoine de Chandieu, whom we will discuss shortly as the third of our key figures.[20]

Around this time in Doornik (= Tournai, in present-day Belgium), where Guido de Brès served as pastor, the community of Reformed believers had grown so significantly that they boldly sang Genevan Psalms in the streets at night, demonstrating their collective strength. Brès, however, did not endorse the public singing of Psalms, recognizing that the government might see it as an act of disobedience or treason—a concern that proved valid. In the preface to the Belgic Confession, he addressed this risk by stressing that true believers should pray for and obey the government, advocating for a peaceful coexistence with the civil authorities. Brès would not have joined in the public singing of Psalms, believing it would only incite trouble. Instead, he took a different approach: in utmost secrecy, he wrote this confession of faith, added a preface, and then courageously had a copy thrown over the castle wall. This was his way of testifying to the government.

Guido de Brès kept his authorship of the Belgian Confession a secret. He instructed one of his closest confidants that if he were captured, the back shed he used as his study—where he kept copies of the confession—should be burned. However, when the authori-

---

20. Gianmarco Braghi, "Between Paris and Geneva: Some Remarks on the Approval of the Gallican Confession (May 1559)," *Journal of Early Modern Christianity* 5:2 (2018), 202.

ties received a tip and came looking for him, the plan to destroy the evidence failed, revealing his secret. Forced to flee once more, Guido escaped with his wife, possibly along with their first child.

Faithfulness to the Gospel and Rejection of the Mass at The Cost of Brès's Life

Guido de Brès could not help but continue to preach the Gospel. Working in several significant French-speaking cities, both the church and his family grew; besides the five cherished children came also numerous books to defend the church's teachings. If you have ever delved into Dutch or Lowlands church history, you will know that 1566 is famously known as the Year of Wonder, marking a significant period of growth and activity for the Reformation. The Year of Wonder, 1566, saw crowds of thousands gathering daily in fields for six to seven weeks to hear the Gospel preached. Brès took part in this preaching. Miraculously, thousands were converted— praise the Lord! However, this widespread public worship drew the attention of the authorities. Consequently, in 1567, Guido de Brès was captured and imprisoned in "The Brunain," a prison's dungeon in Valenciennes, where the sewer flowed by in a channel. Metal cuffs and shackles held him; he wrote to his wife that his wrists were galled to the bones.[21]

From his confinement in the Brunain Guido wrote poignant letters to his wife and mother, which I highly recommend.[22] These

---

21. This letter is published in Cornelius Plantinga Jr., *A Place to Stand: A Study of Ecumenical Creeds and Reformed Confessions* (Faith Alive Resources, 1981), 35.

22. See note 21. See also a translation by Wes Bredenhof, available online. Accessed Nov 10, 2024. See https://dn790004.ca.archive.org/0/items/BredenhofArticles1/AReformationMartyrComfortsHisWife.pdf

letters address some profound questions: How does one cope with the persecution of loved ones while facing one's own death? How do you express love to those you will leave behind? What truly matters in life, and where does comfort lie for both the one persecuted and those left behind? Amazingly, Brès contrasted his own "joy and gladness" with his dear wife's "grief and anguish." He added, "I pray you, my dear and faithful companion, to be glad with me, and to thank the good God for what he is doing, for he does nothing but what is altogether right and good." Brès counted suffering for Christ to show how closely he was united to Christ and thus to fill him with joy.[23]

A month after composing his letters to his wife and mother, Brès was still alive. However, he then faced interrogation by Bishop Richardot, a significant figure in the Roman Catholic hierarchy. This interrogation was crucial, as the record was used to justify the authorities' decision to sentence him to death.

We, in fact, possess the full record of the interrogation.[24] In it Brès demonstrated his profound knowledge of Scripture and early church writers, quoting both from memory with precision. His arguments were compelling, and he remained unwavering in his commitment to truth. When accused by the bishop of valuing his personal judgment over the church's consensus, Guido countered with Scripture references and the early writers. He showed that the Scriptures and the older traditions were not being followed by the contemporary Roman Catholic Church. Brès stated he would accept the Mass and transubstantiation if Jesus had indeed commanded it and if it were biblical.

---

23. Plantinga, *A Place to Stand*, 35.

24. Wes Bredenhof, "De Brès versus Richardot: A Sixteenth-Century Debate Regarding the Lord's Supper," *The Confessional Presbyterian* 6 (2010), 134–47.

The bishop confessed that, left to his own judgment, he might doubt that the actual body of Christ is sacrificed in the Mass. However, he maintained that since the church had settled the matter, it must be believed. This stance reflects the Roman Catholic view where the church's authority shapes biblical interpretation. However, the Reformed perspective, and indeed the biblical one, holds that Scripture, as God's revelation, should dictate church doctrine, not vice versa.

This Roman position was later termed the "coal miner's faith," illustrated by a miner's simple response when asked about his beliefs. The coal miner was asked what he believed, and the conversation proceeded as follows:

Coal Miner: I believe what the church believes.

Question: Well, what does the church believe?

Coal Miner: Why, the church believes what I believe!

Question: Well, then what is it that both you and the church believe?

Coal Miner: Well, we both believe the very same thing!

In this scenario, there is no direct engagement with the Word of God, no personal study of Scripture, no grounding for one's faith. This renders the church lifeless, letting it merely follow the priest's directives without thought. However, this contradicts biblical teaching, as the Lord declares, "You are all a kingdom of priests and a holy nation" (Exo 19:6), "a chosen people, a royal priesthood" (1 Pet 2:9). God calls every believer into a direct relationship with him, through His Word.

You are all called to know God, from the least to the greatest, for His Holy Spirit is poured out on all. Know His Word, find His church, join it, and submit to the yoke of Jesus Christ, serving to build up your brothers and sisters. Brès exemplified this in his Christlike service. This call echoes a continuity from earlier reformers like Farel, whose books often had these words on the title page: "read and judge," in order to encourage personal engagement with scripture.

This approach appeals directly to readers, urging them not to rely on the priest's interpretation or check if books are on a forbidden list. Instead, it calls for personal engagement: "Read it yourself, read God's Word, and judge with Spirit-led discernment whether it is true." This is precisely what Guido de Brès advocated, promoting a faith where each individual is responsible for understanding and applying Scripture.

In the Belgic Confession, Brès describes the church as inherently tied to Christ, an eternal king who must have subjects, emphasizing a faith grounded in God's Word. Specifically, in Article 37, he discusses the final judgment as a profound source of joy and comfort for the righteous, anticipating the completion of their redemption, where they will be rewarded for their labors and sufferings. Our heavenly Father offers profound comfort to his persecuted church.

On May 31, 1567, Guido de Brès and his colleague were sentenced to hanging, not burning as heretics. This is because they were found guilty of treason, having been accused of disobeying the authorities and endangering their country. Despite this, Brès' last words from the scaffold were an admonition to his followers to obey the ordained authorities, showcasing a martyr's commitment to Christian principles even in death. How remarkable from this man supposedly guilty of treason!From Brès's life we can glean valuable lessons, reflecting the broader narrative of the Reformation in Europe, where thousands of stories—pastors, parents, scholars, and even children—illustrate a commitment to faith through suffering. These individuals, in obedience to the Lord, joined His true church, demonstrating a profound allegiance. Like

Brès, they found deep joy in their obedience, despite the trials, highlighting the unity and resilience of the faithful. From Brès and many like him, we learn that commitment to the truth of the Gospel surpasses the value of earthly life. Persecution is an expected part of this commitment. The worst judgment of all—the only one to fear—is God's.

We are all called to know the Lord personally through His Word, striving for Christian maturity. Despite living only to the age of 44, Guido de Brès dedicated his life to studying Scripture, deepening his relationship with God, and understanding the historical confessions of the church.

If we now step back to compare Brès to Farel, we could notice that they died within two years of each other. However, Farel was a first-generation Reformer, much older at death than Brès. Farel's most noteworthy work in advancing the kingdom of Christ was done during the 1520s, 1530s, and 1540s. Brès, however, was a second-generation Refomer. He did his most memorable work in the 1560s. When we compare the Lord's work through these two men, do we see some progress?

On the one hand, the two were very similar. Both held to the same Reformed faith. Both wrote confessions of faith and preached to new converts. Both gathered new churches. On the other hand, advances had occurred. For instance, in the 1550s and 1560s the Roman Church had begun to respond to the Reformed teachings via the Council of Trent; the Jesuit order was coming into existence and quickly developing scholarly acumen against the Reformers; the Anabaptists were gaining converts and deepening theologically with the help of Menno Simons in the Lowlands. Brès faced these opponents, Roman Catholics and Anabaptists—two sides at once.[25] Farel, however, mostly opposed

---

25. On Brès versus the Anabaptists, see Theodore G. Van Raalte, "'Whoever Is of God has the Spirit of God': Children in the Reformation Documents, with Particular Reference to Heinrich Bullinger and Guido de Brès," in *Children and the Church: Do Not*

Roman Catholic teachings. The Council of Trent had decided in the 1540s that the apocryphal books should be counted as true, canonical books of the Bible, and thus Brès did something that Farel, in his prime, hadn't needed to do, that is, to name all the apocryphal and canonical books, as Brés did in articles 4 and 6 of the Belgic Confession. When the Anabaptists needed to be answered, this was a new error, and Farel asked Calvin to do it. In Brès's context and era, the Anabaptist influence was significant enough that Brès opposed them in the Belgic Confession itself more than once. Brès also had in hand a resource that Farel did not have in the earlier era, namely, all the biblical Psalms put to music in the Genevan tunes. And in Brès's time, the Reformed churches were becoming known for this, such that the public singing of these songs would help the authorities and the non-Reformed Europeans know that a good number of Reformed believers were present.

When Richardot interrogated Brès in 1567, the discussion was theologically deeper than when Farel debated, say, Guy Furbity or Pierre Caroli in Geneva in 1534 and 1535.[26] It's not that Brès was more educated than Farel, in fact, quite certainly he was less educated. Yet Brès's context pressed upon him the need to show in more detail that the church fathers were on the side of the Reformed and that the Scriptures opposed the Anabaptists. Brès could also rely upon works like Calvin's Institutes, the likes of which Farel certainly did not have prior to 1536.

Both men shared this fundamental principle: the conviction that the Word of God serves as the foundation for theological argument.

Hinder Them, ed. William Den Hollander and Gerhard H. Visscher (Hamilton, ON: Lucerna CRTS Publications, 2019), 153–79. On Farel debating Anabaptists but afterward asking Calvin to engage their views in writing, see Van Raalte, "Apostle of the Alps," 69, 71.

26. Van Raalte, "Apostle of the Alps," 65–6.

Despite their diverse backgrounds and contexts, they were united in the faith. God was continuing the work of gathering his one, holy, catholic, and apostolic church (as we confess in the Nicene Creed). Having noted this continuity, we can enter into a discussion of our last Reformation pastor-theologian, Antoine de Chandieu.

Later Reformation: Antoine de Chandieu (1534–1591)

Finally, let us consider Antoine de Chandieu (1534-1591), our third figure, whose life spanned a later time in the 16th century.

A Vast Inheritance

Many of the French Huguenots were of the nobility, well-educated and owning estates. Born into nobility, Chandieu faced early adversity when his father died in war, leaving his mother to raise and educate him and his brother. She instilled in them the responsibilities of their vast inheritance, which included multiple castles, extensive lands, and numerous servants managing crops across their estates.

Upon the death of his older brother, Antoine de Chandieu inherited his family's extensive estates, which enabled him to serve as a pastor in Paris from the age of 23 without needing church financial support—he lived off his inheritance. However, this independence was not without its challenges. Records show, for example that in a time when persecution of the Huguenots increased, he sold one estate to a neighbor to prevent the Catholic authorities from seizing it under the pretext of his heresy. When times changed, the neighbor sold it back to him.[27]

Pastoral Ministry in Paris

Antoine de Chandieu likely started his ministry as pastor of the Church in Paris in the spring of 1557, only to be imprisoned in 1558

---

27. Theodore G. Van Raalte, *Antoine de Chandieu; The Silver Horn of Geneva's Reformed Triumvirate* (Oxford: Oxford University Press, 2018), 48–48–59.

for his faith. Remarkably, he was freed the very next day by Antoine de Bourbon, the father of the future King Henry IV of France. Chandieu's fellow prisoner, who hoped to become a pastor, was subjected to six months of interrogations and maltreatment, and was judged to be a heretic. He died, but the next day his body was given a heretic's treatment: it was disinterred and burnt.[28] Some years later, Chandieu wrote a martyrology which included 81 pages about his fellow prisoner. As a nobleman who was rescued by Antoine de Bourbon, Chandieu maintained a close relationship with their family, especially with King Henry VI, in the subsequent years.

Given his noble status, Antoine de Chandieu was frequently called upon by the French Reformed churches to defend their cause before the monarchs. Trained in law at the University of Toulouse, he was known for his disciplined thinking. Additionally, his education included a period akin to boarding school, where he lived with and was mentored by a particular teacher, further honing his intellectual and practical skills. It is truly remarkable how Antoine de Chandieu, despite losing his father at a young age, matured into an exceptionally responsible and capable man.[29]

Antoine de Chandieu, while rigorously trained in law and known for his disciplined, scholastic thinking—scholastic refers positively to accuracy and precision—also possessed a profound poetic talent. His poems, particularly the series Sur la Vanité du Monde, were so celebrated during his lifetime that they were set to music.[30] I have 20th-century recordings of these works, which continue to be performed today, showcasing how his contributions extend beyond academia into the cultural and spiritual life of the church.

Scripture as the Foundation to Theology
We see a recurring theme among Reformation leaders: Guillaume Farel's call to "read the Bible and judge," was echoed in Guido de Brès'

---

28. Van Raalte, *Antoine de Chandieu*, 1–3.

29. Van Raalte, *Antoine de Chandieu*, 42–7.

30. Van Raalte, *Antoine de Chandieu*, 69, 70–71, 77–82, 177–204.

confrontation with Bishop Richardot, where Brès insists on the necessity of a scriptural foundation over mere acceptance of church doctrine. Similarly, Antoine de Chandieu frames Scripture as *principium*,
or *foundation*, for theological argumentation. He uses advanced syllo-
gistic framing of his arguments to show that the Bible, not tradition,
should be the basis of our faith and understanding. Each of these three
figures stood on the same foundation, but their explanation and defense of Scripture as foundation deepened with each generation. The
formation of their arguments sharpened and they paid more attention
to how to teach these points in a more refined academic context.

Chandieu adeptly used hypothetical syllogisms, not merely for
academic debate but to solidify faith's certainty.[31] His treatises tack-
led core issues: defending Scripture against human tradition, affirming Christ's priesthood against the Mass, and clarifying forgiveness against human works and purgatory. These works were
structured for clarity and certainty, grounded in Scripture (cf. 2
Tim 3:16–17), ensuring theological conclusions were derived from
biblical texts. Chandieu also engaged in polemics against Roman
Catholic opponents, particularly Jesuits, whose arguments necessi-
tated a robust Reformed response in his later era. His work was
about defending truth, which, unlike lies, has a firm foundation.
Therefore, he emphasized the need for young men in ministry to
discern and uphold the truth of the Reformed perspective.

Chandieu advanced his arguments by writing out six books in
the 1580s, each one in the format of an advanced academic disputation.[32] He began by asserting his own thesis over against the contra-
dictory thesis. He then sought to show in the next chapter how the
Scriptures truly did provide the solid foundation for the truth of his
thesis. In another chapter he dismantled opposing arguments by

---

31. Van Raalte, *Antoine de Chandieu*, 205–38.

32. Van Raalte, *Antoine de Chandieu*, 77–9; 239–40.

pointing out their errors inasmuch as they failed to rest upon biblical foundations or reasoned fallaciously. This more intricate way of arguing was intended to help Reformed students of theology learn how to walk in true faith, resting upon the Scriptures, and at the same time reasoning with validity. Chandieu's methods of argumentation grew out of a refreshed reading of Aristotle's treatment of logic and careful thought about the best way to craft arguments and strengthen the faith of his readers.

Chandieu's commitment to resting his theological argument on scripture as the foundation was also evidenced in a situation where he was compelled to confront the king for a moral infringement. For many Frenchmen, Henry IV stands as the most beloved king from history. During the tumultuous War of the Three Henrys in the 1580s, one of his chaplains was Antoine de Chandieu. His ministry was impactful, especially when the king, who led their army, had an affair, and fathered a child. Under Chandieu's leadership, the church publicly required the king to confess his sin, which he did. When someone criticized his rigour, Chandieu preached the gospel, emphasizing that "one cannot be too much humiliated before God."[33] This incident showcases Chandieu's commitment to preaching and living a faithful Christian life on the basis of the Word of God, regardless of one's station in life.

Conclusion

In conclusion, the Reformation was a divine act of grace. The Spirit of God brought many sinners back to the truth of the Word of God through all the sharing, preaching, and writing of Reformed believers, particularly of Reformed preachers. The Reformation showcased its catholicity through the diverse yet unified efforts across Europe. The three figures we examined were French-speaking but they each worked in different times and places. More widely, the European Reformation as a whole involved people from all the regions and

---

33. Van Raalte, *Antoine de Chandieu*, 58.

languages of Europe. At large, despite their differences, they were united in faith, reflecting the "one, holy, catholic, and apostolic church." This unity was achieved through many local reform movements, highlighting the international scope that was evident even before Luther's time. The absence of a single leader is clear when we look at figures like Guillaume Farel during the early Reformation, who urged believers to read the Scriptures and judge their contexts on that basis; Guido de Brès in the middle of the Reformation, who worked tirelessly to gather believers around scriptural truth; and Antoine de Chandieu in the later Reformation, who exemplified how to defend the Gospel with both logic and passion.

These individuals illustrate how the Reformation was not led by one person but was a collective journey towards restoring the church to its foundational truths. When it came to presenting the gospel in a coherent and compelling manner, especially for those in ministry, the focus remained on Christ as the full and complete Saviour. Amidst kings and armies at war, national unrest, persecution, and plagues, the Spirit of God made his Word come alive in sinners once again, and gathered together the people who were ready to lay down their lives for him. What God holds paramount in his plans is the advancement of his kingdom through salvation.

Many died for the faith, from pre-Reformation figures like Jan Hus to Reformation heroes like William Tyndale, Thomas Cranmer, and Guido de Brès. They gave their lives to honour God and urge others towards faithfulness. Their martyrdom was part of God's broader strategy, where preaching was the primary means, but many other events were used by God to spread His Word across Europe. Guillaume Farel, Guido de Brès, and Antoine de Chandieu were all Reformed, sharing a common faith yet each playing a unique role in confronting specific opponents. It is a testament to the beauty of God's work that He raised up Reformed believers in diverse locales. We have not even touched on Hungary, where there are also many Reformed individuals. God, through the reading of the Scriptures and the movement of His Spirit, uniquely equipped and positioned these believers in each place to further His Kingdom.

Here we stand today, called to be faithful to the Word of God, blessed by the legacy of those who came before us, to embrace the truth, receive forgiveness of sins, and the gift of the Spirit.

I recall a famous Reformation scholar, an agnostic Jew with whom I briefly studied in Geneva in 2008. He emphasized how the doctrine of predestination, as preached by the Reformers, liberated sinners from guilt and fear. He cautioned historians against reducing their explanation of the embrace of Reformed theology to mere material things like the volume of printed pages, or the number of sermons heard, arguing these metrics alone fail to explain why people were drawn to these beliefs. Instead, he stressed that *the doctrines* preached, prayed, and printed during the explosive growth of Protestant churches were profoundly impactful.[34]

One of the doctrines that this unbelieving historian considered to be important for explaining the "success" of the Reformation was predestination. That's exactly the topic with which I would like to close: God's gracious act of choosing sinners, his election—it's utterly gracious. God's Word is the Gospel, embodying the power of God for the salvation of all who believe (Rom 1:17). This Gospel enters our lives by grace alone, not because we invited it in.

God precedes every good thing, especially our faith. The Apostle Paul teaches us in Romans 8:29 that those whom "God foreknew, he also predestined to be conformed to the image of His Son." The doctrine of predestination has a very long history in the church due to its biblical roots. You can trace it through figures like Augustine or Thomas Aquinas, yet it is peculiarly associated with, and often oddly blamed upon, the Reformed churches.

---

34. Van Raalte, *Early French Reform*, 34–5.

How might this teaching of God's gracious choosing serve as solace for troubled souls, even according to a historian who is an agnostic Jew?

First, it shows that God did not find us already conforming to His Son's image; if He had, there would have been no need for predestination. Instead, God has reset our lives, infused resurrection into our souls, and altered our destiny for eternity, all before time began, independent of any preceding good desire or effort on our part. As Paul writes in Ephesians 1:4, this divine action was set before time.

Second, predestination is comprehensive. It speaks of a new destination being determined for us. As such, it encapsulates the work of the Father, the Son, and the Holy Spirit—encompassing the choosing (Father), the atonement for sin (Son), and the heart's renewal (Spirit). Everything is put in place and taken care of because God has set our final destiny and will not let anything rob us from him.

Third, the term "election," more than any other doctrine, speaks profoundly of grace.

It is about grace because it is about those whom God foreknew and loved. Paul isn't saying in Romans 8:29 that God foreknew what He would decide to do. Of course, God knows all of that. But in Romans 8:29 the Holy Spirit is moving him to say much more. Paul is saying that God foreknew you as a whole, as an entire person, as a sinner—you as the object of His love. Election is the act of God to redirect fundamentally the self-chosen destiny of sinners. This is an act of pure love. Those whom He foreknew, He also predestined. He set their destiny before time, before they existed. But why? Because He had first foreknown them. What kind of knowing is this?

Let me suggest that we should think of it as the counterpart to what Paul prays for us: that we would know the love of God that surpasses knowledge. God's foreknowing is not merely in his head, just like your knowing the love of God isn't just in your head. God knows you with a love that surpasses knowledge. His knowing is the intimate knowing of one who sets his affection on another, like a husband sets his affection on his wife. Now, your wife deserves your affection. But we have no right or claim or goodness that we should be the bride of Christ. God, from the depths of His own heart, found there the love that he could not find in us.

This is the most enduring and stable thing in the whole universe: God found love in his own heart. This love comes only by his grace. It has spread out until all the world was changed for the better. So, the Reformation happened because God predetermined that it would. And now you could rightly say that he has predestined everything. True that is, but the point here is that God was and is all the more intimately involved wherever there is true reformation. His heart is there, his love is being poured out. That is why the three men we looked at, and so many around them and with them, diligently preached the gospel. God moved them to do so. Through them, he graciously and sovereignly administered the merits of Jesus Christ, his Son, to lost sinners. His Spirit moved them to cry out to him in their despair.

And He keeps equipping His servants to live out this gospel, to share this good news, and officially to preach this Gospel. God grants reformation to continue to happen by grace alone.

Map of Europe illustrating the international diversity characterizing the Reformation

Five Key Pre-Reformers (In Black)

Late medieval spiritual deformities
- 1215, Fourth Lateran Council decisions
  ◊ transubstantiation
  ◊ private confession to the priest once/year
  ◊ laity receive mass once/year but only wafer
  ◊ papal primacy proclaimed anew purgatory
- 1274, Council of Lyon affirmations
  ◊ Mary immaculate (free of original sin)
  ◊ prayer to Mary takes root: "Hail Mary, mother of God, pray for us now and in the hour of our death.vAmen." Also, the rosary of either 150 or 50 beads, divided into sets of 10, to keep track of "Hail Mary's" and utter an "Our Father" after every set of 10
- In the mid to late 1400s, emotionalism, superstition, and money-making increase greatly
  ◊ images of Christ on the cross (crucifixes) more contorted and bloodied
  ◊ 14 stations of the cross as aid to worship
  ◊ sacred heart of Jesus and immaculate heart of Mary objects of devotion and art
  ◊ veneration of relics makes lots of money
  ◊ indulgences now available for loved ones in purgatory as well (sell more of them)
  ◊ consecrated host is centre of all worship, made hundreds of times / day upon hundreds of altars in each cathedral
  ◊ leftover consecrated host kept in holy boxes (tabernacles) and held high for display and parade in gilded monstrances
  ◊ many chantries (endowed masses on behalf of the dead, often with special altars and alcoves). E.g., by 1518 the diocese around the city of Geneva had 1435 endowed chantries. At the cusp of the Reformation, in 1536, the cathedral of St. Pierre in Geneva housed 100 chantries, plus 23 altars
- one scholar remarked that the difference between magic and priest's work was hard to discern. Thus "hoc est corpus meum" (this is my body") came to be satirized as "hocus pocus."

Sola Scriptura & Tradition

Dr. David Robinson

THE REFORMATION OF THE sixteenth century was a reformation within the Western Church. Debates about the principle of *sola scriptura* or Scripture alone addressed questions of religious authority and the relationship between Scripture, tradition, the magisterium of the Roman Catholic church, and the papacy. What I want to consider is the principle of *sola scriptura* and the question of religious authority in the correspondence between Lutheran theologians and Jeremiah II, the Patriarch of Constantinople and head of the Eastern Orthodox Church.[1]

The correspondence began in the fall of 1574, when James Andreae (professor of theology at the University of Tübingen) and Martin Crusius (professor of Greek and Latin at Tübingen) sent the Augsburg Confession to Patriarch Jeremiah II in Constantinople. The Augsburg Confession is a Lutheran confession of faith, first published in 1530. Andreae and Crusius describe the Confession as

> a little book that contains the main parts of our entire faith,
> so that your Holiness may see what our religion is, and
> whether we agree with the teaching of the churches under

---

1. Latin and Greek text of the correspondence: *Acta et Scripta Theologorum Wirtembergensium et Patriachae Constantinopolitani* (Witebergae, 1584). English translation of the correspondence: *Augsburg and Constantinople*, trans. George Mastrantonis (Brookline, Mass.: Holy Cross Orthodox Press, 1982).

the jurisdiction of your holiness; or whether perhaps, there might be something that is not in agreement…if it is not too much for your wise person, to kindly express you most favorable judgment concerning these articles, if God would grant that we think alike in Christ.[2]

The Lutherans wrote the Patriarch with the expectation he would not only review but agree with the Augsburg Confession, so that, through his "favorable judgment," the Lutherans and Orthodox might come together in a common confession of faith.

To this end, the Lutherans describe their Confession as a summary of the ancient faith, preserved and passed down through the centuries: "We were in no way innovating on the main articles concerning salvation, since (as far as we know) we held and had kept the faith which was handed down to us by the Holy Apostles and Prophets, by the God-bearing Fathers and Patriarchs, and by the seven Ecumenical Synods that were founded upon the God-given Scriptures."[3] The Lutherans recognized that the Orthodox saw themselves as the faithful heirs and defenders of the ancient Christian faith, and in this initial letter, they claim the same inheritance.

A year and a half later, Jeremiah's commentary on the Confession arrived in Tübingen. The subsequent Lutheran-Orthodox corre-

---

2. *Augsburg and Constantinople*, 27.

3. *Augsburg and Constantinople*, 28-29. The God-bearing Fathers and Patriarchs are bishops and theologians whose writings have been received as orthodox and normative in the Orthodox Church. The ecumenical councils were church councils that met between 325 and 787 to address and rule on various doctrinal and ecclesiastic issues. The confessions, definitions, canons, and anathemas pronounced by these councils are considered normative for the Orthodox Church. The Orthodox reception of the Fathers and the Councils is well-represented by Jeremiah II in his response to the Lutherans.

spondence lasted six years and addressed a variety of theological, liturgical, and ethical concerns, including (1) the procession of the Holy Spirit, (2) the freedom of the will, (3) justification, faith and good works, (4) the nature and number of the sacraments, (5) various ascetic practices and the monastic vocation; (6) and the invocation of the saints.

The dialogue eventually broke down, however, because of a fundamental disagreement on the authority of Tradition (i.e., the exegetical, doctrinal, ethical, and liturgical norms which are set out in the writings of the Fathers and the canons and creeds of the Seven Ecumenical Councils). For the Lutherans, *sola scriptura* was the only standard and rule by which matters of Christian faith and practice are judged. For the Orthodox, Scripture interpreted and mediated by Tradition was normative. My presentation considers this fundamental disagreement over the normative rule of Scripture and Tradition.

First Exchange
Patriarch Jeremiah II to Lutherans (15 May 1576)

On 15 May 1576, Patriarch Jeremiah II sent his commentary on the Augsburg Confession to Tübingen. He begins by stating that there is nothing original in his response to the Lutheran confession:

> In responding, then, we shall say nothing originating of ourselves, but (what is pertinent) from the holy seven Ecumenical Synods with which, as you write, you acquiesce and you accept. We shall further speak in accordance with the opinion of the divine teachers and exegetes of the divinely-inspired Scripture, whom the catholic Church of Christ has received in common accord, for their words and miracles illuminated the universe like the sun. Because the Holy Spirit breathed on them and spoke through them. Indeed,

their statements shall remain unshaken forever because they are founded on the Word of the Lord.[4]

In this opening statement, Jeremiah is clear that he holds a high view of the Scripture; however, he sees the Church Fathers as necessary luminaries, "divine exegetes of the divinely-inspired Scripture."

In the rest of the letter, he comments on each of the Confession's 28 articles. I will briefly consider his commentary on three of them, in order to demonstrate the way in which Tradition informs his response.

First, in Article 4 on justification, the Augsburg confession clearly states that we are freely justified for Christ's sake through faith, without works. The Patriarch agrees that divine assistance leads us down the road to perfection; nevertheless, while "the leading is God's work, to be worthy to be held by his hand depends on our zealous effort. If we are unclean, that hand will not help us. Good works and purity are necessary to acquire divine help."[5] For, as Chrysostom says, "reconciliation is not only believing, one must demonstrate a righteous life and strive after it."[6] And, as Basil the Great says: "the grace from above does not come to the one who is not striving."[7]

Second, Article 7 of the Augsburg Confession defines the one, holy church as the congregation of saints in which the Gospel is rightly taught and the sacraments (baptism and the Lord's supper) rightly administered. Jeremiah responds with his own definition: "One is the holy, catholic, and apostolic Church [which] executes what has been legislated, defined, and determined by the canons, as

---

4. *Augsburg and Constantinople*, 27.

5. *Augsburg and Constantinople*, 40. The Orthodox, following many of the Church Fathers, viewed the work of salvation as synergistic, involving the cooperation of God's grace and human effort.

6. q.v. *Homily 2 on 2 Corinthians*.

7. q.v. *Ascetic Rules*.

given by the Holy Fathers and ratified by the Holy Spirit."[8] Accordingly, the Holy Fathers have established seven, not two sacraments. They are baptism, chrismation, holy communion, ordination, marriage, penance, and holy unction. Although Jeremiah argues that all seven originate in Scripture, in his explanation of chrismation, he cites only Dionysius the Areopagite.

Third, Article 18 on the freedom of the will states that while the human will has some liberty to choose civil righteousness, it has no power to choose the righteousness of God, which is spiritual. The Patriarch agrees that before all else, divine help and grace are needed, for the Lord says, "apart from me you can do nothing" (John 15:5). Nevertheless, Jeremiah adds,

> Yet we hear also the sayings of the holy teachers and exegetes of the divine words of the Lord. These men did not speak for their own purpose, but were moved by the Holy Spirit, and instructed and taught us with the clearness of light. Saint Chrysostom says 'grace, even though it is grace, saves those who are willing.'[9]

Jeremiah then cites long exegetical quotations from Chrysostom's homilies on biblical passages that appear to deny the freedom of the will (mainly, Romans 9:16; Philippians 2:13; Ephesians 2:8). Following these quotations, he exhorts the Lutherans:

> We should keep the ancient customs and obey the interpreters of the Scriptures. Paul spoke in the Holy Spirit, so did Peter and the rest, as well as the hierarchs, Basil the Great, Gregory the Theologian, John Chrysostom, and the remainder of the chorus of teachers. They appear as luminaries in the world, who clearly stated the word of life, proclaiming

---

8. *Augsburg and Constantinople*, 47.

9. *Augsburg and Constantinople*, 78.

the things of our God and most adequately clarifying all of those things for us.[10]

Again, the Fathers serve as luminaries. Scripture needs to be read and interpreted in their light.

Jeremiah concludes his commentary with an invitation to follow patristic tradition:

> All these things which we have spoken, beloved, are founded, as you very well know, upon the inspired Scriptures, according to the interpretation and the sound teaching and explanation of our wise and holy theologians [the Fathers of the Church]. For we may not rely upon our own interpretation and understand and interpret any of the words of the inspired Scripture except in accord with the Fathers who have been approved by the Holy Synods, [inspired] by the Holy Spirit for a pious purpose, lest our thought, like that of Proteus move around here and there, deviating from the correct evangelical teaching, from true wisdom and from prudence. But someone will say, how can these things be corrected? In this way: with the help of God. Let no one undertake or think anything contrary to the decisions of the Holy Apostles and the Holy Synods. He who uprightly keeps this principle will be a partner with us in our rejoicing, a member of our community and one who holds the same faith.[11]

The Lutheran theologians had claimed in their initial correspondence that the Augsburg Confession preserved the faith of the early church. Jeremiah studied their Confession in the light of that very faith and found it wanting. In his commentary on each article, he cites both Scripture and the Fathers. His patristic citations general-

---

10. *Augsburg and Constantinople*, 80.

11. *Augsburg and Constantinople*, 102.

ly concern matters of exegesis and he quotes most extensively (in fact, almost exclusively) Basil the Great (primarily on issues of Christian practice) and John Chrysostom (primarily on matters of Christian doctrine).

Lutheran response to Patriarch Jeremiah II (18 June 1577)

The Lutheran reply to Jeremiah's commentary on the Augsburg Confession was written by Lucas Osiander (professor of theology at Wittenberg) and translated into Greek by Martin Crusius. The tone is respectful and congenial, but apologetic. Osiander introduces his response:

> This is not something we dreamed up, but the true exposition and interpretation of the words received from the Holy Scriptures which with God's help we will present so as to defend our opinion…we believe these truths, which we have learned from the inspired Scriptures through the illumination of the Holy Spirit.[12]

The first section argues that the Word of the Almighty God of all is the standard rule by which all dogmas are ascertained and determined.[13] As the Psalmist says, "Thy law is a lamp unto my feet, and light to my path" (Ps. 119:105), "by which," the Lutherans explain, "he means not opinion and human traditions, but the heavenly, revealed Word of God."[14] In sum: "dogmas should be judged soley by the God-inspired scriptures (*ex solis scripturis sacris*)."[15]

This rule – *sola scriptura* – should be applied in all controversies concerning faith, worship, and practice. It was this rule that the Fathers and the Councils used to refute heresy. As Chrysostom says,

---

12. *Augsburg and Constantinople*, 108.

13. *Augsburg and Constantinople*, 110.

14. *Augsburg and Constantinople*, 110.

15 *Augsburg and Constantinople*, 112; *Acta et Scripta*, 152.

"there is no defence of true Christianity and no other refuge for Christians who wish to know the true content of faith than the divine Scriptures"; and as Basil the Great says, "let the God-inspired Scriptures decide."[16]

This does not mean, therefore, that the Lutherans do not honour the Fathers. On the contrary, "we thank the merciful Lord of all for the exceptional writings of the Fathers which lead to salvation … and we accept and hold in respect all those conciliar decrees which are in harmony with Scripture."[17] Nevertheless, such acceptance and respect is not indiscriminate. There is a difference between the prophets, the Lord, and the apostles on the one hand, and the Fathers and Councils on the other. The latter does not receive equal honour alongside the former. The Fathers and Councils never claimed such status. Just as a stream becomes muddied when it passes through an earthen channel and no longer flows as purely as it did when it first sprung from its source, so the writings of the Fathers and decrees of the Councils have muddied the pure waters of Scripture with the notions and concerns of their historical context.

The Lutherans then argue for the sufficiency of Scripture. The Bible is complete and perfect, so there is no need for the supplementary role of tradition. As Chrysostom says, "the Gospel included everything, things present and things future: life, and godliness, and faith, and all things at once."[18]

What about obscure and difficult passages in Scripture? Is the interpretation of the Fathers not necessary to explain such passages? Indeed, there are difficult passages in the Bible; however, the Lutherans argue, what has been stated obscurely in one place, is stated so explicitly and clearly in another place that the most simple person

16. *Augsburg and Constantinople*, 112.

17. *Augsburg and Constantinople*, 113.

18. *Augsburg and Constantinople*, 115.

can understand it: "Therefore, no better way could ever be found to interpret the Scriptures than that Scripture be interpreted by Scripture, that is, through itself. For the entire Scripture has been dictated by the one and the same Spirit, who best understands his own will and is best able to state his own meaning."[19] The true meaning can be found by comparing passages, provided the reader has first invoked the assistance of the Holy Spirit. This hermeneutic was, the Lutherans point out, the Fathers' own approach to Scripture.[20]

The knowledge of Scripture's original languages is another necessary tool for proper interpretation. Here, the Lutherans say they have an advantage over the Fathers, many of whom could not read Hebrew. Again, they assure the Patriarch that they hold the exegetical labours of the Fathers in high regard; however, "it should not be supposed that they are so indispensable as to imagine that without their explanations and commentaries, it would be impossible to find out, with the guidance of the Holy Spirit, the true and genuine meaning and power of the Scriptures."[21] Just as Christians who lived before the time of the Fathers and Councils read and interpreted the Bible without any risk to their salvation, so too the Bible can be read and understood by anyone of any era who, "in a way befitting the pious and in fear of God, study them without the interpretations of the Fathers."[22]

Having argued for the Scriptures as the only standard and rule for doctrine and life, the Lutherans go on to discuss 16 disputed points of Christian doctrine and practice. I will briefly highlight their arguments on three of them in order to illustrate their application of *sola scriptura*. The disputed points are: (1) the

---

19. *Augsburg and Constantinople*, 115.

20. *Augsburg and Constantinople*, 116.

21. *Augsburg and Constantinople*, 116.

22. *Augsburg and Constantinople*, 117.

freedom of will, (2) justification and good works, and (3) the sacrament of chrismation.

First, while Basil the Great and Chrysostom may have taught that the will is free, Genesis 6:5 clearly states "that every imagination of the heart turns intently toward evil continuously." And again, Paul says that "the mind set on the flesh is hostile to God; it does not submit to God's law, indeed it cannot" (Rom 8:7). The unregenerate or spiritually dead person cannot choose the good on his or her own. The Lutherans nevertheless find support for their position in the writings of both Basil and Chrysostom. Commenting on Galatians 4:9, Basil says, "you have not apprehended Christ because of your virtues; but Christ has apprehended you by his coming" (p.122).[23] Commenting on 1 Corinthians 8.6, Chrysostom says that God has made us believers (p.123).[24]

Second, concerning justification and good works, the issue is not whether Christians should do good works – they should, or whether good works follow faith – they do. The Lutherans' concern is whether good works have any part in the means by which one is reconciled to God and counted among the heirs of God. Is salvation by grace alone, or a cooperation of our good works with divine grace? Their discussion of justification primarily revolves around Pauline texts (esp. Romans 3-4). The mode of appropriating Christ's righteousness is faith alone. Just as the Israelites only had to look upon the bronze serpent to be healed, so we are healed by looking to the crucified Christ through the eyes of faith. Again, the Lutherans provide select quotations from the Fathers (Epiphanius, Basil, Chrysostom, and Gregory of Nazianzus) to support their position.[25]

---

23. *Augsburg and Constantinople*, 122; q.v. Basil, *Homily on Humility.*

24. *Augsburg and Constantinople*, 123; q.v. Chrysostom, *Homily 20 on 1 Corinthians.*

25. *Augsburg and Constantinople*, 126-127.

Third, concerning the sacraments, the Lutherans argue that only baptism and the Lord's Supper are explicitly ordained by Christ. Chrismation receives extended treatment because Jeremiah had only cited Dionysius, the supposed disciple of Paul, in his explanation of the origin of this sacrament.[26] The Lutherans are unconvinced. They find nothing of the apostolic spirit in Dionysius's writings. Besides, he quotes Clement of Alexandria. How then, could he have been a disciple of Paul?[27] Chrismation is nowhere found in Scripture and should not be counted among the church's sacraments.

The Lutherans reiterate their commitment to *sola scriptura* in the epilogue to their letter. What they have written was not derived from their own reasoning, nor are they innovators in any matters of faith; rather, "we believe and teach those things which are written and contained in the books of the Prophets and Apostles. Nothing, indeed, is more ancient, more truthful, more plain, or more steadfast than this teaching."[28]

The Second Exchange
Patriarch Jeremiah II to Lutherans (7 May 1579)

In Jeremiah's second answer to the Lutherans, he does not devote much attention to refuting the Lutheran appeal to *sola scriptura*. He simply states at the outset of his response that his positions on disputed issues are supported by the patristic tradition:

> For it is a stipulation of the holy and Sixth Ecumenical Synod directing that the Holy Scriptures be understood as the tried and proved teachers of the Church have interpreted them and not as those who, by their own sophistry, wish to

---

26. *Augsburg and Constantinople*, 129-130.

27. In other words, the writings attributed to Dionysius the Areopagite are from a much later date (ca. 500). The author of these writing is commonly referred to as "Pseudo-Dionysius."

28. *Augsburg and Constantinople*, 149.

interpret such matters superfluously. Read also the stipulation of the 19th canon: And if any controversy in regard to Scripture shall have been raised, let them not interpret it otherwise than as the luminaries and doctors of the Church have expounded it. And in these let them glory rather than in composing things out of their own heads lest, through their lack of skill, they may depart from what is fitting.[29]

Jeremiah does, however, address the Lutheran concern about the "muddy waters" of the Fathers. In a long discussion on the procession of the Holy Spirit, Jeremiah admits that some Fathers appear to support the *filioque*.[30] The Fathers are fallible, hence the importance of the Councils. Only those Fathers and their writings canonized by the Councils are reliable. Thus, while the writings of Irenaeus, Hippolytus, and Dionysius of Alexandria are admired, not everything they wrote is accepted. The Patriarch adds that the historical context and occasion for which the Fathers wrote cannot be ignored. Sometimes the Fathers speak for the sake of argument.[31]

Nevertheless, the patristic tradition remains canonical. Jeremiah concludes his defence of the veneration of icons with an exhortation to stand within the tradition of the church – "let us not remove the boundaries which our Holy Fathers have set."[32] In the next section, he again exhorts the Lutherans: "Let us accept the tradition of the

---

29. *Augsburg and Constantinople*, 151-152.

30. The *filioque* refers to the addition of the word "filioque" in the Latin translation of the Nicene Creed. Whereas the original Greek version confesses that the Spirit "proceeds from the Father," the Latin version added the word "filioque" which is translated "and the Son." Thus, the Latin version confesses that the Spirit "proceeds from the Father and the Son." Jeremiah II and the Orthodox are adamant that the original Greek version is theologically correct.

31. *Augsburg and Constantinople*, 171.

32. *Augsburg and Constantinople*, 197.

Church with a sincere heart and not a multitude of rationalizations …Let us not allow ourselves to learn a new kind of faith which is condemned by the tradition of the Holy Fathers."[33]

Jeremiah concludes his second response with another invitation to accept the orthodox faith without innovations:

> And since we have agreed on almost all of the main subjects, it is not necessary for you to interpret and understand some of the passages of the Scripture in any other way than that in which the luminaries of the Church and Ecumenical Teachers have interpreted … For nothing else is the cause of dissension than this and only this, which when you correct it, we will be, with the grace of God, in agreement; and we will become one in the Faith, the glory of God. For having researched diligently some of the passages of Holy Scripture, which you referred to in your first and second letters which you sent to us, we saw clearly that you had misinterpreted them, perhaps in following your new teachers. For this reason we again entreat you to understand the passages as the Ecumenical Teachers of the Church have interpreted them and which interpretations the seven ecumenical synods and the other regional ones have ratified. For as we have already said, it is not necessary to rise up and remove everlasting boundaries which the Fathers have established, so that we will not violate the definition which was mentioned at the beginning of the Sixth Synod and be subject to penalties.[34]

Lutheran response to Patriarch Jeremiah II (25 June 1580)

The Lutherans' second reply to Jeremiah was composed by a team of seven theologians from Tübingen and Wittenberg. They would

---

33. *Augsburg and Constantinople*, 198.

34. *Augsburg and Constantinople*, 210.

not budge on their commitment to *sola scriptura*: "we recognize the holy and divinely inspired Scriptures as the only standard and rule (*solam sacram scripturam normam illam atq. regulam*), but which it is necessary to examine all the doctrines of religion and faith."[35] If the Orthodox would only accept this criterion, unity of faith would be achieved.

The Lutherans then marshal the same arguments for *sola scriptura*:

1. Scripture is sufficient and complete, and requires no auxiliary clarification from the Fathers or early church councils.
2. Scripture is clearly understood when passages are collated and compared, and apparent disagreements are resolved with the assistance of the Holy Spirit.
3. Scripture is read with further clarity in its original languages: "return to the sources (*ad fontes*) of the Hebrew language for the Old Testament and the Greek text for the New Testament."[36] The Fathers did not know Hebrew, nor did they appreciate the Hebrew idiom of New Testament Greek.
4. Although the Fathers are not disdained, they do not hold an equal place of honour alongside Christ, the prophets, and the apostles. Christ did not command us to consult the Fathers, but to search the Scriptures.

The Lutherans also argue that patristic exegesis is inconsistent. The Fathers do not always agree with one another. They respond to Jeremiah with their own exhortation: "We entreat your Holiness to enter into the same manner of study with us, and carefully scrutinize and assess the words of the Sacred Writings. Do not tolerate the diverse or opposing interpretations and explanations of the Fathers, which are obstructed and limited."[37] They reiterate

---

35. *Augsburg and Constantinople*, 218-219; *Acta et Scripta*, 265.

36. *Augsburg and Constantinople*, 219; *Acta et Scripta*, 266.

37. *Augsburg and Constantinople*, 223.

the appeal to *sola scriptura* at the end of their letter: "Truly, we believe that the interpretation of the Scriptures, which is the most certain and most secure, is that which makes the Scriptures interpret itself (that is, by dexterously placing the God-inspired words beside each other and comparing them by referring back to the sources of the Hebrew and Greek phrases as the most excellent counselor)."[38]

The Third and Final Exchange
Patriarch Jeremiah II to Lutherans (6 June 1581)
The final exchange is considerably shorter and less congenial than the previous two. The Patriarch concludes his final answer to the Lutherans with a request to be released from the correspondence because the Lutherans do not recognize the authority of the patristic tradition:

> Therefore, we request that from henceforth you do not cause us more grief, nor write to us on the same subject if you should wish to treat these luminaries and theologians of the Church in a different manner. You honour and exalt [the Fathers] in words, but you reject them in deeds. For you try to prove our weapons which are their holy and divine discourses as unsuitable. And it is with these documents that we would have to write and contradict you. Thus, as for you, please release us from these cares.[39]

Lutheran response to Patriarch Jeremiah II (December 1581)
Despite the Patriarch's request, the Lutherans mount one final response, which was composed by an even bigger team of theologians (10) from Tübingen, Wittenburg, and Stuttgart. Concerning the au-

---

38. *Augsburg and Constantinople*, 285.

39. *Augsburg and Constantinople*, 306.

thority of the patristic tradition, they write: "we concede to that authority of the Fathers which they bestowed on themselves, that is, by accepting what they have written insofar as they agree with God-given Scripture."[40] Scripture alone is sufficient: "For only the Word of God (*solum enim Verbum Dei*), in the struggle of man who is afraid, is unconquerable, the only encouragement and strengthening of him who labours and is heavy-laden."[41]

Conclusion: The Only Standard & Rule

Jeremiah II and the Lutherans debated the basic question of religious authority and the relationship of Scripture and Tradition. Jeremiah never questioned the authority of the Scriptures, but he saw the Fathers and the Seven Ecumenical Councils as the necessary mediators of scriptural authority. The Scriptures can only be read and understood in the light of the Fathers and the Councils. For the Lutherans, Scripture can be read and understood in its own light, clear passages illuminating obscure passages, in the light of the original languages, and by the guiding illumination of the Holy Spirit.

The Lutherans initiated the correspondence assuming a shared theological inheritance and thus a kindred spirit. What the correspondence revealed, however, was how Western they were. They proved to be heirs of the Western tradition in their defense of the *filioque* and their appeal to the original sources (*ad fontes*). That they felt a need to clearly distinguish between Tradition and Scripture reveals a more Latin, Western mode of thought.

The Orthodox did not understand why such a clear distinction needed to be made. Why separate Scripture, the source of divine truth, and Tradition, the means by which the Scriptures are faithfully received and passed on? As they would see it, Christians encounter

---

40. *Augsburg and Constantinople*, 313.

41. *Augsburg and Constantinople*, 314.

the Word of God in the liturgy and respond in the ascetical and spiritual life. The form and content of the liturgy and spiritual life were set by the Fathers and the Councils. Tradition mediates the Word of God.

The Lutherans questioned the reliability of Tradition. They warned that the mediation of the Fathers and Councils is not infallible. They conclude their final letter with a pastoral concern: "only the Word of God (*solum enim Verbum Dei*), in the struggle of man who is afraid, is unconquerable, the only encouragement and strengthening of him who labours and is heavy-laden."[42] In the end, it is not the writings of Basil of Caesarea or John Chrysostom that provide such comfort, but only Scripture, only the unconquerable Word of God.

---

42. *Augsburg and Constantinople*, 314; *Acta et Scripta*, 379.

The Principle of *Soli Deo Gloria*

DR. BRIAN G. NAJAPFOUR

*O the depth of the riches both of the wisdom and knowledge of
God! how unsearchable are his judgments, and his ways past
finding out!
For who hath known the mind of the Lord?
or who hath been his counsellor?
Or who hath first given to him, and it shall be recompensed
unto him again?
For of him, and through him, and to him, are all things: to
whom be glory for ever. Amen.*—**Romans 11:33-36 (KJV)**

IN THE 19TH CENTURY, theologians sought to distill the core beliefs of the Protestant Reformers into five concise Latin phrases,
known collectively as *the five solas*:

- *Sola Scriptura*: Scripture alone
- *Sola Fide*: faith alone
- *Sola Gratia*: grace alone
- *Solus Christus*: Christ alone
- *Soli Deo Gloria*: to God alone be the glory.

I will be addressing the last of these five *solas*, that is, *Soli Deo Gloria*.

I begin, first, with a question: Why did *Soli Deo Gloria* become a rallying cry for the Protestant reformers in the 16th century? Did not the Roman Catholics also believe that glory belongs to God alone?

Well, the answer is partially yes and partially no.

Yes, in *theory*, Roman Catholics did, indeed, believe that glory belongs to God alone. However, in *practice*, their explicit denial of the other four *solas* implies that they did not really believe that glory belongs to God alone. Let me explain my point here: The Roman Catholics, for instance, acknowledge that salvation is by grace, but not by grace alone—not *sola gratia* because they reject the doctrine of total depravity. They deny the fact that we, by nature, are spiritually dead. Indeed, we are *so dead* that in and of ourselves there is nothing we can do to save ourselves from sin. The Roman Catholics, however, maintain that there is *something* that we can do to save ourselves from sin—we can somehow contribute to our salvation. Well, if this is the case, then the glory partly goes to God for His grace, and partly to us for our contribution. And yes, the Roman Catholics do affirm that salvation is through faith, but not through faith alone, not *sola fide* because they add good works to faith. And so, according to the Roman Catholics, glory goes to God, the author of faith, and to us, because of our good works. In the Catechism of the Roman Catholic Church, we read this, and I quote, "all men may attain salvation through faith, Baptism and the observance of the Commandments."[1]

Observe, then, that Roman Catholics do not deny the importance of faith in salvation. But the idea that sinners may be saved through faith, baptism, and obedience to God's law contradicts the

---

1. *Catechism of the Catholic Church*, 2nd ed. (Vatican City: Libreria Editrice Vaticana, 1997), para. 2068.

doctrine of *sola fide*. Therefore, while the Roman Catholics may not outright deny *Soli Deo Gloria*, their teaching on salvation suggests that in practice they do not fully uphold the idea of *Soli Deo Gloria*. They do not really believe, in practice, that glory belongs to God alone. For that reason, John Hannah said that Soli Deo Gloria is "the logical implication of the other four" *solas*.[2]

What does this mean? Well, it means that if we embrace *Sola Gratia* (salvation by grace alone), without our contribution; if we embrace *Sola Fide* (salvation through faith alone, apart from our works); if we embrace *Solus Christus* (that salvation can be found exclusively in Jesus alone); if we embrace *Sola Scriptura* (that Scripture alone is our final supreme authority in life and doctrine), then it logically follows that all glory belongs to God alone. As David VanDrunen explained, *Soli Deo Gloria* is "the glue that holds the other [four] *solas*" together.[3]

What I will thus do in my remaining time is study this Latin phrase, *Soli Deo Gloria*, in light of the text of Romans 11:36. Let me restate that verse: "For of him, and through him, and to him, *are* all things: to whom *be* glory for ever. Amen." I want to make three observations from our text—notice the three prepositions here, *of*, *through*, and *to*.

- "For *of* him are all things": God is the *source* of all things.
- "And *through* him": God is the *agent* of all things.
- "And *to* him are all things": God is the *goal* of all things.

God is the *Source* of All Things

In Romans 11:36, the Greek preposition ἐξ (*of*), which can be translated as "from" or "out of ", is used to indicate the origin or source of all things.

---

2. John D. Hannah, *How Do We Glorify God?* (Phillipsburg, NJ: P&R, 2000), 9.

3. David VanDrunen, *God's Glory Alone: The Majestic Heart of the Christian Faith* (Grand Rapids, MI: Zondervan, 2015), 14-16.

In other words, what Paul is saying here is that God is the *origin* of all things. All things came out of Him. Now let me clarify that statement: when we say that God is the origin of all things, by "all things", we are not saying that God is the origin of evil. James makes it clear in James 1:13 that God is not the source of evil—sin did not originate from God. It originated from Satan, the author of evil. And so, the "all things" in our text should be qualified by what James says in James 1:17, "Every good gift and every perfect gift is from above and comes down from the Father of lights." Put differently, when we say all things, we're talking about all good, perfect things, including our salvation. Salvation originated from God, or *in* God. In fact, when we carefully look at the literary context of our text, the entire chapter of Romans 11, you will see that the apostle Paul is talking about the things pertaining to our salvation.

And so, when Paul says, "for of Him [of God] are all things", he is particularly talking about salvation—things pertaining to our salvation, such as faith, which comes from our God. And that is why he calls it a gift from God. He says this in Ephesians 2:8, "For by grace you have been saved through faith, and that not of yourselves; it is the gift of God (NKJV)." Faith is the means by which we receive Christ's perfect righteousness. This perfect righteousness—absolutely essential, without which no one can stand before a holy God—is the very thing we lack, and the very thing God graciously provides.

We need that righteousness to be imputed to us through faith in Christ, for without it, no one can be justified in His sight. And that righteousness comes from our God.

And this is the amazing truth: when God gave us His Son, He also graciously provided the very means by which we receive Him and all His saving benefits. The means is faith—a gift of grace itself.

Let me illustrate the point. Imagine you're very hungry—it's supper time. And out of mercy, I give you food—a warm bowl of soup. Wonderful! I've provided what you need to satisfy your hunger. But I don't stop there. I also hand you a spoon—an instrument to help you eat and enjoy that soup. In that context, the spoon serves as the means by which you receive the nourishment provided. The same is true when it comes to faith. We often say "our faith," but in reality, that faith comes from God—it is His gift to us. The reason we believe in Jesus is not because we produced faith on our own, but because God graciously gave it. So, not only did He give us salvation, but He also provided the instrument—faith—by which we receive it.

Now, obviously, we are not saved by faith in itself—faith cannot save us. It is the object of our faith, the Lord Jesus Christ, who saves us. Everything in salvation comes from God, even repentance. If we repent of our sin, if we see sin as God sees it, that is a gift from God. That conviction that we have whenever we sin, and when we are convicted by the Holy Spirit, we know very well that it is a gift from God—"of him are all things"—all things pertaining to our redemption. In Acts 11:18, we read, "When they [the brethren in Jerusalem] heard these things [how the Gentiles had received God's Word] ... they glorified God, saying, 'Then God has also granted to the Gentiles repentance to life.'" Notice here that it is God who has granted repentance to the Gentiles, a repentance leading to life. And that is why Jonah can say this in Jonah 2:9, "Salvation is of the Lord." Salvation belongs to God. Salvation originates from God. Salvation does not originate from us.

Consider this example: as a writer, when I quote a statement that is not my own, I must acknowledge the original author. I do this by citing the source—perhaps in a footnote—giving credit where credit is due. In the same way, our salvation is not original to us. It does not come from us, and therefore, we must acknowledge its true Author—the source of our redemption, our God.

Even the very plan of our salvation originates with Him. By nature, you didn't even want to be saved. How could you? As fallen human beings, we are not just morally weak—we are totally depraved. Not partially, but totally. As Paul says in Ephesians 2:1, we were spiritually "dead in trespasses and sins."

That's why we need the sovereign work of the Holy Spirit. He is the one who has quickened our dead souls, bringing us to life. He has opened our hearts to the gospel—this is the only reason we can now see and savor the beauty and glory of the Lord Jesus Christ.

We also did not plan for our salvation—God did, from eternity past. The triune God purposed our salvation before the foundation of the world. The Father chose a people to save and sent His Son to redeem them; the Son willingly undertook to accomplish their redemption through His perfect obedience and sacrificial death; and the Holy Spirit applies the benefits of Christ's finished work to the elect in time. This eternal covenant reflects the perfect unity and purpose of the Godhead in bringing about our salvation. There you can see that salvation from start to finish is the work of our triune God.

In Revelation 7:9–10 John saw in a vision "a great multitude which no one could number, of all nations, tribes, peoples, and tongues, standing before the throne and before the Lamb, clothed with white robes, with palm branches in their hands, and crying out with a loud voice, saying, 'Salvation belongs to our God who sits on the throne, and to the Lamb!'"

You see, all the saints will be crying out some day with a loud voice. We'll be saying,

> "Salvation belongs to our God who sits on the throne,
> and to the lamb, the Lord Jesus Christ."

Now, in Roman Catholic theology, salvation is partially a result of human effort. Salvation partially belongs to man because, for the Roman Catholic Church, we can contribute to our salvation, and so we can take credit for our salvation and therefore glory in ourselves— the glory is split between God and us.

But we say with the reformers, *Soli Deo Gloria*, to God alone be the glory. There is no boasting, as Paul says. And that is why, if you are a true child of God, your life should be marked by humility. Humility is a fruit of saving grace and a true expression of thankfulness. If you truly acknowledge that salvation belongs to God, then you must also recognize that it does not originate in you. It is not something inherent to you—it has been graciously given by our merciful God. And when that truth grips your heart, the proper response is one of humble gratitude: "Lord, thank You. Thank You for the glorious gift of redemption that I have in Jesus Christ. Thank You for this double gift—not only did You give me salvation, but You also gave me the instrument through which I receive it: faith in Christ."

God is the *Agent* of All Things

The second observation in our text is this: God is the agent of all things. Notice again what Paul says in Romans 11:36: "…for of Him and through Him…"—*through Him are all things.*

Now, let me ask you: what is the difference between the prepositions "of" and "through" in this verse? Is there a meaningful distinction between them?

Yes, there is. As I mentioned earlier, the preposition "of" (or "from" or "out of") indicates that God is the source or origin of all things. But when Paul says "through Him," that preposition points to God as the agent—the one through whom all things come into being. In other words, it is God who not only designs salvation, but also actively initiates and accomplishes it.

And we see this truth from the very beginning. When our first parents fell into sin, who took the initiative to restore the relationship? It wasn't Adam and Eve—they didn't seek after God. In fact, they hid from Him. It was God who came to them. God pursued Adam and Eve while they were in hiding.

This pattern holds true throughout redemptive history: in salvation, it is always God who takes the initiative. Who gave His Son? It was God. As John 3:16 declares, "For God so loved the world that He gave His only begotten Son." We didn't ask for the Son. You didn't ask for Jesus. You didn't even ask for salvation. How could you? According to Scripture, you were dead in trespasses and sins, unable to seek God on your own (Eph. 2:1; Rom. 3:11).

Who then came into the world to seek and to save the lost? It was Jesus. And Christ came, not because we sought Him, but because He came to seek and to save us—lost, helpless, and undeserving sinners such as we are (Lk. 19:10).

And that is why Paul can say in Philippians 1:6, "being confident of this very thing, that He [oh, I love this verse!] who has begun a good work in you will complete it until the day of Jesus Christ." So, who began the work of salvation in us? It was God—because He is the agent of all things, and "through Him are all things."

That preposition "through" not only implies that God is the initiator of our salvation, but also that He is the active *doer*—the one who carries it out from beginning to end. This is why, when Paul speaks of salvation, it is consistently expressed in the passive voice. In English grammar, we distinguish between the active voice (where the subject performs the action) and the passive voice (where the subject receives the action). Consider Ephesians 2:8: "…for by grace you have been saved…"—that's passive. It tells us that we are not the ones doing the saving—we are the ones being saved. God is the one who acts. We simply receive.

And by the way, to believe in Jesus Christ is a command. Throughout Scripture, we encounter imperatives like: "*Seek the Lord while He may be found,*" or "*Call upon the name of the Lord, and you shall be saved.*" These are commands.

But here's the striking reality: we who are totally depraved—we who are dead in sin—are being commanded by God to seek Him. We who are lost are being called to look for Jesus. And we can only respond because God, by His Spirit, gives us life and enables us to obey.

And so, when we believe in Jesus, we know very well that it is the work of God. It is the work of our God because the gospel imperative comes with His grace. Therefore, when Paul says, "Believe in the Lord Jesus Christ, and you will be saved," if you believe, it is because you have been given His grace to believe. He is the doer—the worker—of our salvation.

But that preposition *through* has also the idea of maintaining or sustaining. To put it another way, when Paul says, "and through Him are all things," he's saying that God is *sustaining* all things. The very earth on which we live is being sustained by God. And that is why it is not collapsing right now—He is upholding it; He is sustaining us, and the same is true when it comes to our salvation.

It is God who maintains our salvation. I am glad that I myself do not maintain my salvation, because I cannot even maintain my lawn, or even my garden. It is hard to keep up! Also, it is hard to maintain our house—there are always things to do. How, then, can you maintain your salvation? Well, we do not have to, because it is God who will maintain it for you. "...and through Him are all things." And that is why our salvation is guaranteed. Because God is going to preserve. On that point, one of the five points of Calvinism has the title, "the perseverance of the saints." In other words, if you are a true saint, a true child of God, you are going to persevere until the end. But I actually love, or prefer, the expression the *preservation* of the saints, because the reason why we're going to persevere is because God is going to *preserve* us. He is going to make sure that Satan cannot pluck us out of His hand. He will make sure that we will be able to cross the Jordan River, and beyond that river is this celestial city where only righteousness dwells. I have this confidence: no matter what happens, even if this world were to be turned upside down, I know I will make it, I know I am going to reach the finish line, I know I am going to see Jesus, because God is going to *preserve* me. Asaph had that realization in Psalm 73. "I am continuing because you are holding me. You are holding my hand."

I have five kids, and whenever we're about to cross a road—a busy, dangerous street—I always make sure to hold their hands. Sometimes one of them will say, "Daddy, you don't need to hold my hand. I can do it."

And I'll respond, "No, no—it's dangerous. I'll hold your hand."

That's how it is with God. He is holding our hand—and He will not let go. We are safe, not because of our grip on Him, but because of His grip on us. As the hymn says, "He will hold me fast."

This is why we have what I like to call a lifetime warranty—eternal security.

When you buy a new phone or laptop, the store might offer a warranty—but it mostly only lasts a year. After that, if something breaks, you're on your own. You have to fix it. You have to maintain it.

But that's not how it works with our salvation. Our warranty doesn't expire—it's eternal. God Himself has guaranteed it. As Scripture says, "Through Him are all things."

Remember the three tenses of our salvation. Ephesians 2:8 stresses that we have been saved. There is a sense that the work of salvation has been completed. We are not partially saved. We are saved! And yet, on the other hand, Paul talks about this progressive tense in 1 Corinthians 15:2 that we are being saved. In what sense? Well, in the sense that we are being sanctified by God. So, we have *been* saved and are *being* saved by God, being sustained, being conformed to the image of our Lord and Savior Jesus Christ.

And then, Paul talks about the future tense of our salvation in Romans 5:9 "…and we will be saved"—that is our glorification; it is guaranteed, as John the Beloved says, "when we see Jesus, we will be like Him." And that is why, again, Paul can say this in Philippians 1:6, "being confident of this very thing, that he who has begun a good work in you will complete it until the day of Jesus Christ."

I was recently in Serbia for a pastors' conference. Serbia is going through financial hardship, and I noticed many unfinished buildings throughout the area. I remember asking one of the locals, "Why are there so many unfinished structures?" He replied, "Well, they began the work, but they went over budget—no money! So they couldn't finish the project."

But God is not like that. When He begins a work, He brings it to completion. He began the work of salvation in you, and He has promised to finish it. He *will* complete it. And you *will* be changed. You will be conformed to the image of our Lord and Savior, Jesus Christ.

Now, in the Roman Catholic Church, that is not what we see. Who maintains salvation in the Roman Catholic Church? It is not really God, it is you. You have to perform good works to maintain your salvation. You need to participate in the sacraments; you have to do this and that, or else you will not make it, or else your salvation will not be complete. And that is why there is really no assurance of salvation in Roman Catholic theology. Even the Pope dies with no assurance. Imagine that! Because the question is, how do you know that you have done enough to secure your salvation? How do you know?

So, you see, I know that I will make it to the end because my God Himself will preserve me. God Himself will provide all that is necessary for my salvation, sanctification, and glorification, as "through Him are all things."

God is the *Goal* of All Things

Now, finally, we have this proposition *to*. Look again at our text, Romans 11:36, for *of* Him—so that is a source—God is our source, the Source of all things. And *through* Him—God is the *agent* through whom all things come into existence. And *to* Him. The preposition *to* indicates the point to which *all things culminate.* In short, God is the goal of all things. God is the final point to which all things end. And here is the beauty of redemption. So, *of* Him or *from* Him—salvation begins with God. And *to* Him, salvation ends with God. And between the two prepositions, between the preposition *of* and the preposition *to* is the preposition *through*—God is sustaining us.

You see, God is the ultimate purpose and reason of all things. Everything that God does, He does for His glory. The very reason why He saved you was for His glory—that is why salvation is not about us—salvation is all about God. What is the chief purpose of God? Why does God exist? Well, we can say for God to glorify Himself and to enjoy Himself forever—"and to him are all things."And when we go back to our text and look at the context, yes, election is for God's glory because Paul talks about election here in Romans 11, but he also talks about reprobation, the hardening of the hearts. And you might ask, why is God hardening the hearts of the wicked? Why did He harden the heart of Pharaoh? Now, of course, we may not know all the details, all the reasonings behind that. But this we know for sure, that He hardened Pharaoh's heart for His glory. The Puritan Nehemiah Rogers said, "Yea, God will have glory by reprobates, though it be nothing to their ease and though He be not glorified of them, yet He will glorify Himself in them." I love that quote! God is going to glorify Himself in the reprobates—He created hell for His glory. He's going to glorify Himself in those wicked, ungodly people who will be spending their eternity in the lake of fire. It is all for His glory.

And so, as Paul reflects on the doctrines of salvation, election, and reprobation, he bursts into praise in Romans 11:33–36, proclaiming:

> O the depth of the riches both of the wisdom and knowledge of God! how unsearchable are his judgments, and his ways past finding out! For who has known the mind of the Lord? or who has been his counsellor? Or who has first given to him, and it shall be recompensed unto him again? For of him, and through him, and to him, are all things: to whom be glory for ever. Amen.

God's knowledge and wisdom are so deep that it is utterly impossible for us to explain His decisions and His judgments. There is no way for us to fully grasp His ways. As God says in Isaiah 55:8–9, "For my thoughts *are* not your thoughts, neither are your ways my ways, saith the LORD. For as the heavens are higher than the earth, so are my ways higher than your ways, and my thoughts than your thoughts."

And the context of that passage—which we often quote—is actually about salvation.

What God is saying is this: when it comes to redemption, His ways are higher than ours. We cannot fully comprehend what God is doing.

Paul asks, "Does God need a counselor?" And yet, sometimes we think we have it all figured out. We try to explain reprobation and election—as if we can peer into the infinite, eternal mind of God. But we cannot. To understand God fully and comprehensively is an impossibility. For that, we would need to *be* God.

But God is God, and we are human beings.

And yet, we know this: all things are *for His glory*. As Paul says, "To Him are all things."

This is where faith must be exercised. This is where we say, "Lord, I don't understand. It doesn't make sense to me. Yet I trust You, Lord, knowing that all You do is for Your glory."

I don't know what kind of trials or afflictions you're facing right now. Perhaps it's cancer, a struggling marriage, health issues, financial burdens, or conflict in your church. Whatever it is—remember this: all things are working together for good. Yes, for *our* eternal good, but also for *His* glory.

You might ask, "Why did God create a spider?" Again—*for His glory.* Why did He allow a hurricane to strike Florida, taking lives and destroying homes? For His glory.

Why did *you* have that accident? We call it an accident, but in truth, it was part of His eternal decree. Nothing happens by chance. Why did He allow this trial in your life? *For His glory.*

You might say, "I don't get it!" And I understand—there are many things in *my* life I don't understand either.

Nevertheless, I bow before God and say: "Oh, the depth of the riches both of the wisdom and knowledge of God! How unsearchable are His judgments, and His ways past finding out. For *of* Him, and *through* Him, and *to* Him are all things. To Him be glory forever. Amen."

You see, our response is to be, "to whom be glory forever, Amen." Someone once said, "the ultimate Reason of everything in the world and work of grace, is the glory of God"[4] And the word glory here in Greek is δόξα (*doxa*), from which we have the English word *doxology*. We often sing that well-known line from the doxology: "Praise God, from whom all blessings flow." And truly, this should be our proper response. The Lord has saved us. He has given us all that we need for our sanctification, all the means of grace for us to grow. And He has guaranteed our future, our glorification. Our proper response is to say, "Lord, thank You. Hallelujah! To God be the glory. Great things

---

4. R.M. Edgar's homiletic and expository notes on Romans 11:33–36 in *The Pulpit Commentary.*

He has done." After all, what is our chief end? To glorify God and to enjoy Him forever.

This precious doctrine of *Soli Deo Gloria* does not promote antinomianism. Some might say, "Well, if salvation is God's work from start to finish, then I might as well just sit down and be passive!" No, no—you do not understand salvation if that is how you respond to God.

Remember what Jesus says: "Let your light so shine before men, that they may see your good works." Yes, we are called to do good works—not in order to be saved, but because we *are* saved. Why? So that others may see your good works and give glory to your Father in heaven (Matt. 5:16).

So that your officemates, your neighbors, your unbelieving relatives—when they look at your life—will be compelled to ask, "Why are you different from everyone else here?"

In that moment, you are letting your testimony shine. And you can say, "Well, it's because of what Jesus has done in my life."

Puritan pastor Anthony Burgess once said, "The love to God's glory should be preferred before ours; we are to desire His glory principally, and our salvation as subordinate." That's quite something to consider. Yes, we long to be saved. We look forward to glorification. But first and foremost, our greatest desire should be for God's glory—not our own. That must be the motto of our hearts. This is why Paul exhorts us, "Whatever you do, do all to the glory of God" (1 Cor. 10:31).

Let me close with an illustration about Johann Sebastian Bach, the great German composer and musician of the Baroque period. Bach once said, "The aim and final end of all music should be none other than the glory of God and the refreshment of the soul."

To those of you who are musicians—let this be your motto. Whether you play the organ, the piano, or lift your voice in song, do it all for the glory of God. And for us pastors, may the same motto guide us: that we preach for the glory of God, that we write for His glory, and that all we do be to His praise alone.

If you are a mother, care for your children to the glory of God. Cook to the glory of God. If you are a father, work to the glory of God. Whatever your calling—do it all for His glory.

At the outset of his musical works, Johann Sebastian Bach would often write the initials "J.J." standing for *Jesu Juva*—Latin for "Jesus, help me." Upon completing them, he would write "S.D.G." which stands for *Soli Deo Gloria*. The psalmist says, "Not unto us, O Lord, not unto us, but to Your name give glory, because of Your mercy, because of Your truth" (Ps. 115:1). We echo the words of John the Baptist: "He [Christ] must increase, but I must decrease" (Jn. 3:30). My prayer is that throughout this conference, God's name would be glorified, and that the Lord would humble each of us—bringing us low to the dust as we lift up and exalt His holy and majestic name. And with one voice, may we all sing with Fanny Crosby: "To God be the glory, great things He has done!"

S.D.G.—*Soli Deo Gloria*

Name Index

Subject Index

Contributors

Kasey Horvath

Rev. Kasey Horvath serves as the Lead Pastor of All Saints Church in Lancaster, Pennsylvania leading as the primary preacher and shepherd of pastoral care. As an Ordained Minister in The Communion of Reformed Evangelical Churches, his pulpit and pen are devoted to instructing the heart and mind of his audience through the teaching and counseling of Holy Scripture.

Steven R. Martins

Rev. Steven R. Martins is the founding director of the Cántaro Institute and founding pastor of Sevilla Chapel in St. Catharines. He holds a Master's degree summa cum laude in Theological Studies with a focus on Christian apologetics from Veritas International University (Santa Ana, CA, USA). He is the General Editor of the *Old Spanish Reformers* series, has translated several sixteenth-century works of the Spanish Protestant reformers, and has authored and coedited numerous books, including *Apologetics* and *La Fuente: Iberoamerican Journal for Christian Worldview*. Steven is married to Cindy, and they live in the Niagara region with their four children.

Theodore G. Van Raalte

Dr. Theodore G. Van Raalte is professor of Ecclesiology at the Canadian Reformed Theological Seminary, prior to which he served as a pastor for eleven years. He completed a Ph.D. at Calvin Theological Seminary in historical theology, focusing on Antoine de Chandieu's (1534-1591) clear presentation of Reformed theology by the use of scholastic method. He is the author of several books, including *As You See the Day Approaching: Reformed Perspectives on the Last Things*.

David Robinson

Dr. David Robinson is senior pastor at Westminster Chapel (Toronto, Canada), an adjunct professor in the Biblical Studies and Theology department at Tyndale University College & Seminary, and presently serves as chairman of the ETS Ontario-Quebec region. His research interests include early North African Christianity and the history of biblical interpretation, particularly the book of Revelation. David has published articles in *Studia Patristica, Worship, Theoforum, Humanitas*, and *Revista Vida y Espiritualidad*.

Brian G. Najapfour

Born and reared in the Philippines, Dr. Brian G. Najapfour holds a Master of Theology from Puritan Reformed Theological Seminary, and a Ph.D. from Theological University of Apeldoorn. He has been a minister of the gospel since 2001 and has served both in the Philippines and in the U.S. He now lives in Canada, pastoring Heritage Reformed Congregation of Jordan, Ontario. He has authored and coedited numerous books and has contributed several articles to journals, periodicals, and encyclopedias.

ABOUT THE CÁNTARO INSTITUTE

Inheriting, Informing, Inspiring

Cántaro Institute is a reformed evangelical organization committed to advancing the Christian worldview for the reformation and renewal of the church and culture.

We believe that as the Christian church returns to the fount of the Scriptures as its ultimate authority for all knowledge and life, and wisely applies God's truth to every aspect of life, its missiological activity will result not only in the renewal of the human person but also in the reformation of culture—an inevitable outcome when the true scope and nature of the gospel are made known and applied.

www.ingramcontent.com/pod-product-compliance
Lightning Source LLC
Chambersburg PA
CBHW051217120626
46547CB00013B/1396